THE MODERN MOVEMENT IN PAINTING

THE MODERN MOVEMENT IN PAINTING

By T. W. EARP

SPECIAL SPRING NUMBER OF THE STUDIO
Edited by C. G. Holme
1935

5

LONDON: THE STUDIO LTD., 44, LEICESTER SQ., W.C.2.
NEW YORK: THE STUDIO PUBLICATIONS, INC., 381 FOURTH AV.

Reg. U.S. Pat. Off.
Printed in Great Britain
by Edmund Evans, Ltd., Globe Road, London, E.1.

CONTENTS

LIST OF THE COLOUR PLATES

EDITORIAL INTRODUCTION

THE modern movement in painting has now become a part of modern history. It is not a tendency but something that has happened. The heat of controversy has died down. Certain proportions begin to appear: a recognizable beginning, a form in what was previously confused: a rounding-off in recent years as the original impetus reached its final stage.

The cooling and solidifying of the æsthetic nebula indicated the need for something in the way of geography—a book that would plot out the ground, would show the reasons for the movement, its peaks and depressions, how far it has set its mould on thought and (as far as we can see) on the future: whether its influence has on the whole been beneficial or otherwise, and in what, actually, the influence has consisted.

Mr. T. W. Earp has undertaken this task in the present volume: and his qualifications for it are considerable. A man of letters, of wide but discriminating sympathy, he has lived in Paris during the development of the modern movement and come into personal contact with the painters and writers who were in the forefront. He is able both to see their work in proper perspective and to speak with the authority of first-hand knowledge: with the aim of informing the intelligent layman rather than of adding to the already considerable corpus of panegyric or abuse.

The illustrations are in colour throughout: as is only reasonable in view of the essential part that colour plays in modern painting. As far as we know there is no existing work already so illustrated, which in itself provides a strong reason for the publication of this book. Monotone plates give only a faint indication of the originals:

but colour reproduction permits a fairly exact appreciation of the artist's aim: and our colour plates have been carefully chosen from the best collections of London and Paris.

The reactions of the modern movement have been so wide-flung, its influence on design so powerful, that it is hoped this careful selection will prove of value not only to painters and students of painting but to manufacturers and designers in industry who may find in it the actual source of many motives of decoration in use at the present day in a more or less garbled form: as well as a heightened sense of the value of colour and form in themselves.

Chapter One: PAINTING AND PARIS

LIKE other articles that are submitted to commercial transaction and change of ownership, pictures are subject to the process of supply and demand. Their creation may be the spontaneous expression of the artist, without any afterthought regarding their disposal, or it may be a deliberate means towards his gaining a livelihood; but in any case it will receive an impetus from the increase in numbers of those likely to appreciate it and possibly to acquire the work produced. Such an increase occurred at the beginning of the nineteenth century and has been maintained, with very little interruption, to the present day.

It sprang from the industrial and commercial development which followed, after an interval of severe economic stress, the close of the Napoleonic wars. Wealth and culture, which in the different countries had been the privileges of a restricted class, became more generally disseminated among the progressive nations. There was a rapid growth in the sections of society capable of aesthetic enjoyment and possessed of the opportunities for obtaining it. Painting profited along with the other arts. Instead of being confined largely to the adornment of public buildings and aristocratic mansions, the demand for it, whether as decoration or portraiture, increased enormously. A swiftly-expanding bourgeois class, whatever the merits of its taste, had become art-conscious.

The fauna of pedagogy received an addition in the drawing-master of young ladies' academies. Aspects of the picturesque, in the smudgy medium of sepia, covered the leaves of innumerable sketching-albums. Taking the place of the young nobleman and his bear-leader, prosperous middle-class families converged *en masse* upon Italy, to visit the monuments and works of art. It was inevitable that with so extended a growth of interest in the works of the old masters, and the rise of the amateur, the professional artist of the day would also benefit. Contemporary production, from the life-size to the miniature, was stimulated, and the ranks of the painters swelled. But while soon even small towns had their local artist, and each state its institution for the encouragement of national production, an international centre of artistic training, creation and commerce, was gradually being formed. By the end of the nineteenth century Paris had established itself in this position, one that it was peculiarly fitted to assume.

Facility and tradition combined to elect it to the function. From outside France it was the first halting stage of European travel, and frequently the goal in itself. It had raised to a high development the business of entertaining the foreign visitor. In the mere spectacle of their daily existence the inhabitants, not altogether unconsciously, provided an attraction. The amenities were meticulously cultivated, while opportunities for pleasure and expenditure were the object of an exquisite organisation. A glimpse of the artist's life, itself a distinctive feature of the city, was a part of the sightseer's routine if he had pretensions to taste. If he had also the means, there was every likelihood of his buying a picture. Besides the native market for his work, Paris offered the painter that of the visiting connoisseur as well. In addition, it gave him opportunities for the pursuit of his profession more favourable than those of other capitals.

Although France had been obliged to return Napoleon's spoils of conquest which had been housed in the Louvre, that palace still provided a superb collection of the world's masterpieces. The royal house of France were not only for centuries collectors of classic art, they, and by their example aristocratic and wealthy families, had actively encouraged the artists of their own time. This official recognition of works of art as a prominent part of the nation's product, and of the artist's particular status as a member of the community, was unbroken by the Revolution. Napoleon and his successors continued it until, in the romantic eighteen thirties, the position of the artist in Paris was not only established but consolidated.

A popular impression, made articulate in Murger's novel, *La Vie de Bohème*, attributed an existence different from that of the ordinary member of society to the writers, artists and musicians of Paris at that period. It was, supposedly, a life ruled by invincible sentimentality, clouded briefly by hardship and sorrow, but on the whole careless and happy, where financial difficulties were pressing, but ignored or ultimately overcome; where, above all, to be a Bohemian was to be some one apart, cast in a finer mould than the rest of the world. The general public, always charmed by romance round the corner, fostered this legend. The subjects of it consciously adopted it, or, while dissenting, were not unwilling to utilise its advantages. Among them the painter, made still more a being of mystery by the possession of a studio and the employment of a model, found his fellow-citizens ready, and indeed eager, to treat him with tolerance and respect.

It is not surprising, therefore, that with this sympathetic environment Paris showed considerable painting activity under the Second Empire. The student had a liberal choice of official or independent art-schools for a training-ground. This maturer work received ample attention from a Press curbed by censorship in its political expression, and in consequence able to devote the more space to picture-exhibitions along with other topics equally harmless from the governmental point of view. And the government itself, directly inspired by the Emperor, inaugurated, along with the annual official *Salon,* a show of the pictures to which that body had denied admission, known as the *Salon des Refusés*.

The intended object of this exhibition of the Rejected was to demonstrate to the public how just had been the choice of the State jury for the Salon itself. Actually, it served a splendid purpose in drawing attention to those painters who were attempting something different from the academic routine. As a result, although these *Salons des Refusés* were abandoned towards the close of the Second Empire, when Parisian life again took on its normal course after the Franco-Prussian war and the Commune, the unorthodox found dealers willing to show their work and the official *Salon* more frequent in its acceptance. The most important of them were a group known under the Third Republic as the Impressionists, of whom Manet was the recognised leader.

The term Impressionist, which was first applied by a satirical critic, is not altogether satisfactory, yet it defines a certain identity shared by all the members of the new movement. Their work, whether in portraiture, figure-group or landscape, possessed an instantaneous quality, the feeling of natural pose caught in a single moment, or of a scene delivering itself at one brief instant to the view, instead of the rigid permanence which their predecessors had for the most part conveyed. In subject-pictures it was distinguished by a choice of themes from the aspects of everyday life instead of mythology, history or romantic fantasy.

But Impressionism has by now been extended in meaning to denote also a technical aim which these new painters held in common, which was a definite departure in the process of picture-making. Instead of presenting objects as rising starkly in an atmospheric void, with gradations of light occupying spaces of the canvas as though they were material layers coating the object behind them, the Impressionists endeavoured, with more fidelity to appearances, to depict light as bathing rather than blotting what it embraced.

These innovations did not win their way without having at first to meet the liveliest disapproval. Aware that the influence of art is far-reaching, although impalpable and not easily defined, that there is somehow a connection between the painted picture and the usages and appliances of existence, with perhaps the subconscious survival of an old belief in a magical property attending representation in imagery, a public, which is mainly indifferent to art, yet resents departure from normal artistic production. Where novelty in the realm of the practical, which has but to undergo the easy test of convenience, is welcomed, in the realm of imaginative creation or representation it is looked upon askance.

Impressionism was a battle-ground with the odds heavily against the Impressionists. Authority, controlling official purchases, reprobated them as members of the Opposition. The academic painters saw in them a detestable heresy and a possible encroachment on their monopoly. The Parisian public, feeling that they were a smirch upon the city's reputation as a patroness of art, followed suit. Only by force of character, by ardour and a supreme faith in themselves, did they conquer in the end.

Since his work caused the most scandal, the leadership of the group was attributed to Manet. Bourgeois by descent and temperament, of a reserved and diffident character, he was popularly regarded as little better than a criminal, and at any rate a danger to society. Much of his work was in the direct tradition of approved masters of the past, while in the theory of Impressionism he did not advance so far as several of his fellows. But he showed the objects in his pictures as though a natural light were playing upon them, instead of subjecting them to an arbitrary pictorial convention of illumination. He painted flesh as it indeed looked, and not as if it were varnished with pink and cream. The true cause of his offence lay in his realism.

Degas was another Impressionist who did not accept all the technical implications attaching to the term. Without covering so wide a range as Manet, but going further in realism, he made the breach between the new and the old painting still more profound. Combining at first the man of fashion with the artist, in the end the latter gained possession and he withdrew into a seclusion of tireless labour and misanthropy. Much of his work is devoted to the complicated artifice of the ballet, to the dancers at exercise or resting behind the scenes, as well as to the illuminated splendour of the performance itself. There, as in his studies of washerwomen and nudes, any concession to prettiness is almost cruelly avoided. Awkward gesture, angular physique and the sad hues of weary flesh are a testimony to the shortcomings of the human form, yet from his stern fidelity Degas creates an enchantment of colour. The appearances in themselves are ugly, but the painter's truth to his vision of them transmutes them into beauty on the canvas.

Renoir merged into Impressionism the clear outlines he brought from his craft of a painter on porcelain. A realist, he took advantage of the new technique to attain more accurate effects of movement, light and colour, though he confined his truth to life to its more gentle aspects. Besides the sparkle of woodland and meadow and the irridescence of the Seine, he painted Parisian work-girls, theatre-parties, dancing couples, young women at the piano, and children. Charm and grace are his characteristics as an Impressionist, but his more original contribution to modern painting is a matter for later consideration and is not limited by the boundaries of the group.

The member of the group who pursued its theories most continuously and intensely was Monet. His early paintings of ladies in crinolines moving through the bright variety of gardens are characterised by the exactitude of one whose eye was a natural camera. But with the development of an exceptional power of analytic vision, the object itself, which was the tangible goal of representation, receded more and more. There was a moral implication in the censure visited on Manet and Degas; Monet's crime was his technique alone. He aggravated it with brave impenitence in the course of innumerable garden-pictures and landscapes—for he was a painter of Nature rather than of cities or figures—and in various series of subjects which show a scientists' delight in their exhaustive examination of particular appearances under changing conditions. Those of Rouen Cathedral, the Thames, poplars, mills, and, in his last years, the water-lilies of his garden, show his analysis of atmosphere growing ever more complicated and yet precise, ever richer in pictorial incident. In the purest sense of the term, he was the Impressionist *par excellence*.

It was a paradoxical movement, demanding strength to attain the tenuous, and almost a discipline of imprecision to render exactitude. The men of determination who were its leaders took a long time to conquer public prejudice against their innovations. By steadily ignoring it, they did much to disarm the criticism which defends what is established without taking the pains to investigate what is new; such criticism is at once the most violent and the weakest. They were aided also by the polemics in their favour of some members of the Naturalist School, whose efforts towards realism in literature were akin to theirs in painting. The most prominent of these allies were Zola, Huysmans and Geffroy. At the same time, in Paris itself, awaking from the illusions of the Second Empire and the nightmare of the siege, a spirit of revision was gaining ground which not merely distrusted artistic as well as political doctrine that had flourished under the old regime, but was anxious to replace it by more scientific investigation and new lines of approach. As this tendency gathered force and became generally acknowledged, it was perceived that, in their particular art, the Impressionists had been moving in unison with it. Their battle was won at last, and in its reconciliation with the rebellious group, Paris, which still remained a focus of attraction, became the capital of modern painting.

Chapter Two : THE POST-IMPRESSIONISTS

AT the Impressionist exhibition of 1874 a few pictures had been shown, signed by a certain Paul Cézanne. They had little in common with the work of the accredited members of the School, and seemed indeed, to the unaccustomed eyes of the spectators, to have achieved an ugliness of their own. A few ungainly nudes and angular still-lifes, their utter lack of interest made them worse than scandalous. It was a satisfaction to know that the official Salon had rejected this painter's efforts with automatic regularity. Recognition was much slower in coming to him than to his fellow-exhibitors, yet the painting of the following century was for many years to be dominated by his name.

Cézanne was that exceptional thing, a taciturn Provençal. He took little part in the eager discussion of the artists' cafés in the Pigalle-Clichy neighbourhood at the foot of Montmartre, for it was necessary to him to work out his meaning to himself in silence and solitude. He renounced the conquest of Paris to return to his native Aix, where, though the townspeople ignored him or laughed at him, he was at least free from the confusion of opposing creeds in art and could explore his own mind without disturbance. Entirely absorbed in his elected task, he remained a happy outcast for the rest of his life.

Atmosphere, the capture of the moment, even accurate representation, in the meaning of representing surface-appearances only, did not interest him. He was a derivation from the old academic school, and not from Impressionism, in that he painted from an idea of the object, rather than from the object itself, as it stood before him. But the idea with which the object supplied him was created by it, and confined entirely to it, whereas the academicians had made it the vehicle for ideas brought from outside, from their conceptions already formed of the beau-ideal, the heroic or pathetic type in figure, the literary or dramatic in group, the romantic or picturesque in landscape, the pretty or abundant in still-life. The object for them was a symbol fitting in with a conception external to itself. But for Cézanne the object made its own symbol, a pattern of form and colour which he perceived within it, which was its very essence.

Thus he painted essential shapes, bringing out relations of mass or volume, of approaching or receding planes of space, instead of contenting himself with surface and outline and approximate indications of distance and measurement. If what he was painting differed in some points of outward form from the authoritative form which he saw within it, then those divergences were irrelevant for him, and sacrificed.

Within the picture there must be nothing that did not contribute to the unity imposed. He asserted the right of painting over Nature, for the ends of painting alone. Banishing all other intrusive, extraneous arts, he revolutionised the attitude of his own to the world before it.

His reduction of shape into its formal elements brought the sections of his composition very near to the basic figures of three-dimensional form, the cube, the sphere, the cone and the cylinder. Here again his origins in academicism showed themselves, but with the vital difference that the old painting took these figures merely as a point of departure in technical exercise, and rarely returned to them, just as too many of Cézanne's imitators have never got away from them. For if Cézanne dissected form in order to build up from it anew, his fresh statement, through dealing with them brusquely, never betrayed the inherent truth, or individuality, of those aspects of Nature upon which he worked. He dominated it, compelled it to his aim, and the result was a union of its pictorial qualities with his visual conception. What was essential in those properties he scrupulously regarded. Not all can be Cézannes who choose, by ruthlessly following his analytic method to the destruction of their share in the picture of the appearances on which the method is exercised, or, as too frequently happens, by being satisfied with analysis alone and forgetting Cézanne's supreme gift of colour.

The humidity in the atmosphere of Normandy and the outskirts of Paris, where the Impressionists accomplished much of their landscape painting, by blurring saliences and casting an almost imperceptible veil over the scene, lent itself peculiarly to their manner. In the same way the country of Provence, with its outlines accentuated and its mass-formation easily defined in the clear air, was altogether appropriate to, and perhaps in some degree suggested, Cézanne's discoveries. At any rate, in spite of the self-criticism that he applied with merciless severity, he worked there with a facility that he had never found in the days of wearisome painting-out and repainting over the same canvas that he had known in Paris. The region of Aix sprang into exquisite new being under his creation, radiant in colour through the variations of the Provencal year. He painted nude groups of a majestic simplicity, before which the pseudo-nymphs of the official schools withered into outworn conventionalism ; in the portraits of himself and the folk about him he illuminated a homely beauty with the enthusiasm of a science unknown before. And in his studies of flowers and fruit he instilled a vibrant life of form into what had become an exercise in virtuosity. Working unencouraged and alone, he was an ascetic with gifts of abundance.

Meanwhile in Paris, where he was for the most part either forgotten or unknown, Impressionism was developing. Pursuing an elaborate theory of optics, Seurat had advanced it to Pointillism. To represent irridescence and the perpetual quivering of light and the resultant instability to the vision of what they played upon, he carried the division of colour still further and refused line as a means of defining form. Instead of using strokes, he covered his canvas with an infinity of small spots of paint, which merged outlines and at the same time disintegrated expanses of colour into their component elements. This gave a curiously dream-like quality to his work, or perhaps rather an early cinematographic effect. His figures flicker into being ; they do not stand already placed before the spectator as entities independent of each other and their surroundings ; the individual features of his landscapes stand out only gradually from the palpitating mirage in which they are interwoven. But the sense of motion or vibration, though at a slower pace than actuality, is complete ; and the suave panellings of colour, lighted and suffused with points, like corpuscles, of a more vivid tint in the same key, attain a pictorial cohesion of great charm in spite of the atomic method by which they are produced.

Seurat was a Parisian of the Parisians, and delighted to portray those amusements of the capital which were especially characteristic of his fellow-citizens and his epoch. His pictures of shows and circuses, and boating-parties and picnics down the Seine, testify to the delight he took in the enjoyments of the people. There is a zest about them which is more than the detached observer's. Like many others of the painters of his time, he worked also on the Normandy coast, mostly choosing lighthouses and breakwaters for his subject. On these he displayed his manner in its most persuasive and least sensational aspect, attaining harmonies of colour, which, for all the novelty of their method, have a classic calm and finality.

He was not only the discoverer of his kingdom ; he explored and possessed it entirely. Pointillism might be called a one-man method—its inventor's. An unsuccessful attempt to imitate him could produce but a bad Seurat, while a successful one at best would be no more than an imitation Seurat. Yet a school—for French painting runs to schools—soon gathered round what could only be an isolated phenomenon. Of these Pointillists, as they were called, one indeed achieved something more than pastiche.

A young Dutchman, Vincent Van Gogh, had come to Paris to adopt the career of a painter, after much painful indecision whether he should not rather follow that of a missionary. With strong religious leanings, and very tenacious of purpose, his intensity had disconcerted the congregations to whom, as an evangelist, he had addressed himself in Holland and Belgium. He was not one who lived easily in contact with his fellows. Painting had been revealed to him as an alternative vocation, and his relations with art-masters and artists at Antwerp and the Hague proved as unsatisfactory as with the miners and peasants among whom he had lived and preached. But after a long struggle, in which he looked upon art and faith as two rivals for the possession of his soul, he at last saw that they were not irreconcilables ; the first might be put to the service of the second. The glorification of the visible world through his gift of painting, by illustrating the beauty of form and colour, might be salvation to himself and the spring of thanksgiving to his fellows. He came to the conclusion that it was unnecessary for his pictures to bear a moral implication, like those of Millet, whom he had spent some time in imitating. It would be sufficient that they should be satisfactory as works of art. And it is a sign of the position that Paris had by then assumed as an art-capital, that he naturally bent his steps there in order to seek perfection in his craft. It is true that his brother, who was also his protector throughout a stormy existence, lived there, but, as he himself said, it was above all to enjoy the communion of other painters that he made the journey.

His very sincerity, however, was so strongly tinged with passion that it made communion difficult. He was only wearied by café discussions and professional shop-talk. Yet with his arrival in Paris his work ceased to be that of an amateur sub-Millet. Colour glowed upon his canvas and his drawing lost its awkwardness. The swift, darting method of Seurat suited the violence of his spirit, for he introduced into his adaptation of it a violence which is not to be found in Seurat's own work. Instead of applying his spots of colour with an even conscientiousness, he gave them a swift turn, a rapid print of eagerness, as they met the canvas, which developed them into a series of quick, short strokes. But he was also strongly influenced by the masters of the Japanese colour-print, whose art had just begun to be appreciated in Paris. In the course of his painting in the city and its suburbs, he evolved a manner which compounded the Japanese and the pointillist methods. The composition and the outlines of the picture—one might say, its gesture—showed Japanese origin ; the execution, the painting within the outlined spatial limits, was in the brief, repeated strokes which bear the undeniable impress of his hand.

He stayed in Paris only a short time. Contact with his fellow-painters revealed a whirlpool of antagonisms instead of the generous enthusiasm of a common effort. He needed escape, and thought that he should find calm and inspiration in Provence. Settling at Arles, in that town and the surrounding country, working feverishly with little thought of his health, he achieved the mastery to which a tormented life had been the apprenticeship. But illness, poverty and continual self-doubt drove him into lunacy, and suicide followed.

That Van Gogh was a religious painter, that he attached to his painting a significance for himself more great than merely the production of a work of art, does not invalidate an aesthetic judgment on it, but it helps an understanding of its passionate emphasis. Once he was in full possession of his technique, he infused into it an ardour that was often excessive, though never empty or rhetorical. There are landscapes where Nature writhes in a cataclysm, portraits and still-lifes distorted with the force of their expression. Yet even in his excesses he displays so profound a delight in natural form, and seizes with such ardour the sudden revelations of colour which the visible world presented to him, that his pictorial statement always imposes the conviction from which it sprang.

One of the few among other artists with whom he had been able to enter into sympathetic relations was Paul Gauguin, though a visit that Gauguin paid him at Arles had only brought two explosive forces into closer contact and precipitated his mental collapse. But their painting, over a short period, shows reciprocal influences. This was not surprising in Gauguin's case, for he was catholic in adaptation. Indeed, his interest largely consists in the wide range of creation from which he drew his own. He was an explorer of styles, and a pioneer in the direction which he investigated with best result.

European painting had hitherto developed along the main lines of European tradition. Gauguin looked further afield. A business-man, he began by practising art in his spare time, as what was called a "Sunday painter;" gradually he devoted all his time and spirit to its exercise. His curiosity was inexhaustible, and to it was added a large share of the doubtful gift of versatility. In his early work are traces of the masters of the Italian renaissance, particularly Botticelli; of his contemporaries, Degas influenced him the most, while, like Van Gogh, he also underwent the attraction of the Japanese. A sojourn at Pont-Aven introduced him to the primitive charm of the religious statuary of Brittany, the archaic figures of its calvaries and the rough-hewn images of saints. This induced a distinct trend to simplification of design and primitivism in conception, which marks the pictures of his maturity.

It was a psychological as well as an artistic inclination. He was one of the founders of that primitive-exotic movement of protest and escape, which has since found so many adherents. Quitting the complications of European existence, he went off to Tahiti, both to paint and live, as far as possible, the native life. There he became involved in local politics, quarrelling with the French officials, uncompromising in conduct and opinion, and dying in misery. But while his experiment was far from a practical success, it was an important event in the history of modern painting. In spite of the difficulties that harassed him, he still contrived to send canvas after canvas to Paris. To a discerning few, whose numbers slowly increased, the exile's work, though disconcerting, made a very forceful impression, which was aided by the efforts of the symbolist poet, Charles Morice.

For a reaction was taking place against the materialist doctrine, which, through philosophy and political theory as well as art and literature, was imprinting itself strongly upon the national mind. It was voiced by the Symbolist School, which found its happiest expression in the medium of poetry, but to which the other arts also contributed. It had, too, its implications in its adherents' attitude to life, upholding the dream and the pursuit of emotional experience as opposed to a realistic concentration upon actuality. Gauguin's paintings, though definitely the product of an individual and deliberately isolated impulse, were never the less extremely appropriate to the symbolist canon. They typified a bold abandonment of everyday contemporary life in capitals; they were detached from associations of modernity.

The remoteness of the South Seas invested them with a dream-suggestion that was often accentuated by an archaism borrowed from the native sculpture. The rich colour was applied smoothly, in panels of lustrous paint. In the very method of Gauguin's painting there was something suavely sensual, with an undertone of savagery, and this impression was borne out by the subjects which he chose. His figures were types of physical beauty, graceful and noble in form; the scenery in which they were placed was tropically exuberant in shape and hue. All that was picturesque in his environment, he projected to its highest power upon his canvas. Sometimes there was a harking back to the Italians in the hieratic posing that he affected; but more often he subjected his composition and the gesture of his design to a compression that was naïvely barbaric, yet controlled, and, in accordance to the traditions of Polynesian art, classical.

That there could be a classicism outside the academic pastiche of the old masters was one of the shocks of revelation administered by Gauguin to his contemporaries. His departure to a land then more or less unknown, and his existence there as painter-beachcomber was another. By his individualism, and by the element of discovery in his work, he was a valuable contributor to the renaissance in art which Post-Impressionism brought about.

For Post-Impressionism was not a school, but an impulse. Its leaders were isolated personalities, all showing a dynamic force of expression, but with very little in common beyond dissatisfaction with official tradition. They all started from Impressionism, but each developed beyond it on independent lines. Seurat, the scientist of technique, influenced a phase of Van Gogh's work. For a short time Van Gogh, the apostle of emotion in painting, and Gauguin, the electric, reciprocally contributed to the perfecting of each other's style. Gauguin, again, was aware of Cézanne's efforts in the simplification of form; though the Provençal painter, who was to mean so much to a later generation, was for his contemporaries the least regarded of them all.

It was as individuals, and not with conscious unity, that they brought a fresh vision to their art and enlarged the range of its expression. Not only in the method of their treatment, technically speaking, but in their method of confronting the visible world before them, they effected a revolutionary change. By their ardent concentration, and the spirit of analysis which reinforced it, it may even be said that they invented a new way of seeing. Previously, with the exception of the impressionist protest, the artist had regarded his subject with a ready-made plan of traditional picturesque in his head, to which, willy-nilly, it had to conform. The post-impressionists gave the subject its freedom, allowed it to rise before them altogether apart from any prearranged conception of it. They enriched Nature with a new wonder.

But another force—this time anonymous—was working in conjunction with them to make theirs a period of renaissance. The monopoly of the purely European tradition for European painting had been broken down. As the only field of suggestion which the artist might explore with regard to style, and as containing within itself all that admitted of the spectator's appreciation, the old masters of the various European schools had dominated exclusively. Work produced elsewhere was either considered barbarous, or at best, a curiosity. By the last quarter of the nineteenth century, however, means of communication had greatly increased; there was more interest, fostered by commercialism, in far-off lands; and philosophic tolerance had enormously broadened. (Buddhism, it may be remarked, was an acknowledged component of the symbolist attitude.)

Thus the art of other continents began to receive sympathetic attention; it was recognised that there might be something in the point of view from which they were accomplished that could be usefully adapted to the modern European spirit. Japanese colour-prints were among the first productions to force their way through the ban, and we have seen them aiding Post-Impressionism towards self-realisation. Gauguin found much to utilise in Polynesian art. It was the first step in opening up new realms of aesthetic appreciation, a process still gaining impetus and still unexhausted. Its inception, and the new kind of analytic vision practised by the post-impressionists, brought about the modern renaissance.

Chapter Three: FROM FAUVE TO CUBIST

POST-IMPRESSIONISM was not only a movement of individuals; it was also, with the exception of Seurat, non-Parisian in the most important part of its achievement. Though its leaders had passed through the capital, and received either the beginning or some portion of their training in it, their real development took place in solitude, quite detached from any metropolitan impulse. But their work had to come to Paris for exhibition and dispersal. It was there that discussion raged around it, and that the succeeding generation of painters gradually absorbed its influence.

This generation was essentially urban. Artists came in increasing numbers from other countries to swell its ranks, bringing in their train a dilettante horde existing on the fringes of the profession. Montmartre became the quarter of their predilection. It was already a pleasure-quarter; restaurants, theatres, dancing-establishments and cabarets, thickly clustered together, catered with notable efficiency for a never-ceasing flow of seekers after nocturnal amusement. A follower of Degas, Toulouse-Lautrec, in a series of brilliant paintings of Montmartre night-life, had, as it were, sealed the union of art and entertainment in this particular district. Certain it is that, whether by an easy relaxation of the sterner problems of existence, a humanitarian sympathy, or because the one could avail itself of a wealth of subjects provided by the other, the two were mutually encouraging.

In what came out of the quarter that was of importance in the painting of the time, the quarter's imprint is perceptible. It is evident not only in subject, but also in a gay daring that characterises its treatment. A new kind of picturesque was evolved, that carried with it a different attitude in the artist when viewing his material, as well as when dealing with it. Detail was regarded much more ruthlessly, salient features were emphasised to the extent of deliberate distortion if such means aided the pictorial effect. The element of caricature, or at any rate of wit, was admitted in serious work. Reserve in choice of subject was abandoned, realism in presentation pushed as far as the painter cared.

The old standard of the beautiful was abolished. Beauty was no longer a necessary component of what was painted, but only of the resultant painting itself. The post-impressionists, in this respect, had preserved the traditional canon that a thing must be beautiful in itself to admit of beauty beng produced from it. They dwelt with loving care upon the aesthetic qualities inherent in their subject, though they used new methods to draw them out on the canvas. Their successors, in some cases as much from fear of the suspicion of sympathy with old-fashioned prettinesses as from courage, often purposely elaborated themes that on their own account possessed little that was gracious or even interesting. It was the triumph of technique over subject.

The painters who adopted the new manner with the greatest eagerness soon had a name attached to them ; not inappropriately they were dubbed *Les Fauves*, or " The Wild Men." The most important survivors of the group have now moved a long way from their original orbit, and will need later consideration from the point of view of their mature accomplishment. It will be seen then that their early fauvist period, for all its truculence and eccentricity, was not without its value in their development.

For Fauvism was a movement of liberation. Everything, pictorially speaking, was permissible, so long as it was new and experimental. Thus whatever spark of individuality a young painter might have had, which would have been stamped out under the more austere traditions previously prevailing, was able to grow to flame if it contained any vitality at all. And from this intense phase of testing and exploration, the art of painting itself received an impetus. It was no longer the depressing vista of a road only too well-trodden that opened before the artist, and a question of spending his life in the repetition, with but slight deviation, of former accomplishment. And the gallery-goer, disconcerted and even alarmed though he might be, at least knew that the Fauves would provide him with excitement, and that painting could offer him more than the wearisome monotony of the official Salons.

And as the philosophy of art follows the creation of art, so the Fauves' demonstration that they did not need inherent beauty in a subject, in order to make beauty out of it, greatly widened the sphere of aesthetic appreciation. The spectator had to admit that a Fauvist picture, say, of a labelled wine-bottle and a thick glass half-filled with a purplish liquid, was beautiful as a combination of line and colour, though these objects were displayed at a curious angle, and apparently slipping from the table on which they stood. When Chardin had painted the same kind of subject in the eighteenth century, the result was also beautiful. But in his case, the glass was of charming shape and workmanship, containing a glowing ruby free from all suggestion of poisonous adulteration ; and instead of a coarsely-standardised bottle was a flask of graceful fashioning. Not only did the " properties " of his picture carry aesthetic weight in themselves, before transmutation into terms of art ; to the nineteenth-century spectator a wealth of association aided their effect as well. In the fauvist version, whatever non-pictorial implication might be read into the canvas was a negative one. Social degradation and a feeling of physical discomfort were the suggestions evoked by it as a representation of reality. Yet as a creation in line and colour it was independent of the reproductional origin from which it came, and could take its place by the side of Chardin's work.

If, then, so-called " ugly " objects could be made into, or could contribute to the making of, beautiful works of art, it would become a natural inclination on the part of the spectator, if only because happiness is more sought after than unhappiness, to consider their visual capabilities of beauty as an artist would. So long as his relation with them was purely visual too, he would find the enjoyment of adopting the Fauves' attitude to them aesthetically overcome the sense of a duty to view them from association-qualities and prevent his dwelling on their ugliness in themselves. Coaxed into using his own artist's vision upon visible appearances, he became aware of a new sense of delight, of a changed world.

Thus the Fauve, by interpreting unaccustomed subjects into terms of art, encouraged those who were not necessarily painters to perform a similar process mentally and for their own satisfaction. He showed that beauty is not some objective, absolute phenomenon, of which the inimitable laws and conditions could be laid down, changelessly manifest and external to humanity. For him, it was possible to create it and not merely copy it.

It was active rather than passive ; it was " the pleasure of seeing " instead of " that which pleases when seen." Above all, it was a process achieving its end in its very exercise, a kind of creative recognition. For the Fauve, the secondary result was the work of art ; although this process that he revealed could be accomplished by anyone, using any aspect of appearances as a starting-point of suggestion. Then, from it, could be elaborated such a conscious arrangement of form and colour in the mind as should give pleasure by its conception. Though colour, it may be remarked, did not need to have any greater importance than as line, marking the boundaries of form. Thus Fauvism was the expression in art of a beauty, which all might fashion in their own manner, and its manifestations were as various and anarchic as might be expected from so liberal a basis.

The example of the Post-Impressionists in the direction of technical liberation was followed, and diversified in innumerable ways, by the Fauves. The fact of their being an urban group no doubt intensified their zest for experiment, and the exercise of it on so many novel subjects, which produced the particular aesthetic revelation that has just been mentioned. A great increase in the production of still-lifes resulted. Van Gogh had demonstrated the pictorial excitement to be obtained from painting a very ordinary chair. The Fauves went far beyond, as happy to work on a leek as on a rose, and bending the most haphazard objects of common use to their purpose They exploited them from unexpected angles of vision, forced them into linear pattern by strange proximities, and ruthlessly altered the shapes of actuality in order to bring out latent pictorial relationships in composition. There was a strong element of neo-romanticism in the movement, in the manner in which they distorted the external world to make it suit their aesthetic emotion. But they pursued this aim with a minuteness and universality that much exceeded the earlier Romantics' artistic transformation of reality. For where the latter sought emotional cohesion, the Fauves were impelled by the spirit of analysis, and the dissolving of entities into particles before they moulded them again into formal expression.

In their spirit, as well as their method, was something of a romantic revival too. The quarter of Montmartre, which was their environment and on which they drew largely for their subjects, reinforced the romantic impulse with its curious admixture of pleasure and misery, of tragedy and theatricality, and the turning of night into day. It offered a macabre contrast of glare and shade. Once the lamp-lit dazzle of the main thoroughfares was left behind, roads of a tortuous complexity ascended the hill. They were for the most part narrow, dark and deserted, where "Fauves," in the social rather than the artistic sense, took their predatory and even murderous ways. They cast an atmosphere of risk, debauchery and obscure intoxication. It is not to be wondered at that many of the paintings of the district convey a feeling of the lurid and the bizarre.

Apart from painting, those whom they elected as masters exemplified personally a strangeness and revolt from the normal that are characteristic of romanticism. Gauguin, who was especially the group's patron saint at the beginning, did so in an eminent degree. And besides the other post-impressionist leaders, they turned admiringly towards Monticelli, who lived out a life of visions and potations at Marseilles during the Second Empire, tortured by a despairing passion for the Empress Eugénie, who painted murky dream-compositions in thick layers of gem-like colour, oddly reminiscent of the *fêtes-champêtres* of Watteau and the bacchanals of Rubens. The Fauves' predecessor in the quarter, and *par excellence* the painter of Montmartre, Toulouse-Lautrec, also influenced them, in his choice of subject and lack of convention in outlook. A crippled dwarf, the scion of a noble and ancient family, he devoted himself to the study of the quarter's pleasure establishments, and particularly the Ball of the *Moulin Rouge*, mingling intimately in the existence of their dancers and frequenters.

In enumerating earlier painters with whom the Fauves discovered affinity, Gustave Moreau demands inclusion. Living from 1826 to 1898, he yet remained aloof from the conflicting artistic movements of the century. Even the actual life about him, in an era of turbulence and change, brought little distraction to his self-centred temperament, devoted to the perfection of a very individual talent. The Italian masters, Rembrandt and Delacroix were his great admirations; his dreams, which besides his work, were his chief activity, moved in a past of classic legend. The passion of Herodias, the adventures of Jason and the Trojan epic are typical of the themes which occupied Moreau's imagination. He displayed them in pictures that have something of the effect of stained-glass windows, so flecked are they with a diversity of brilliant colour, so shot with irradiations of light and chasms of shade.

Many of them were water-colours, which he elaborated on a larger scale to form designs for tapestry. Among the pupils and employees in his studio, connected with this department of his work, was Georges Rouault, the *doyen* and leader of the Fauves, if painters so eminently personal and developing in such various directions can be said to have had a leader. Rouault adopted much of Moreau's method, but turned it towards very opposed purposes of representation. His painting is a setting of jewels that gleam through darkness, but instead of a grace of form and dreams, he paints the brutal shapes of a barbarous modernity, seeking in contemporary life the savage and truculent expressions of human character. His figures are awkward, with a Romanesque bulk in their mass; the line that bounds them is thick and deliberately clumsy. They are, viewed as portraiture, often of a revolting ugliness; for there is in Rouault, a distinct element of harsh satire. But he invests them with a magical depth of colour, a richness of hue that either sparkles dazzlingly, or in whose gloom are lambent tongues of buried fire. Some of the pictures are a devastating exhibition of the nullity and hideousness of the *petit bourgeois*, others a cry of horror at the degradation of lust; but there are also robust exultations in the lively, simple joy of fairs and circuses, where colour takes on the stridency of brazen instruments of music, or laughs with the ferocious fun of clowns.

No greater contrast could be found to Rouault among the Fauves than the early Matisse. With him, a volatile, elastic line whirled in adroit arabesque about splashes of colour that were bright indeed, and yet possessed the impalpable qualities of essences. Suggestion and rapidity of notation could hardly be reduced to a finer point, than in the work of Matisse at this period. Blank spaces are left in the canvas when what has already been painted sufficiently indicates how the composition would be completed, or when the main pictorial assertion that has been made would only be confused by further additions. Often, too, when it has been shown that a pattern, say, of a dress or a curtain, is continuous, it is left incomplete. For the Fauvist æsthetics, of which we have spoken, not only gave the spectator the faculty of becoming an artist himself, although non-executive; it admitted him to collaboration mentally in carrying out its conceptions. Matisse pushed this aspect to its extreme in the logic and economy which exercise so rigid a control over his apparent haphazard. Colour and the freedom of colour being his object, he saw no need to give more than a minimum of delineation to hint at an imitation of reality, which was not really his aim, once it had ceased to be an excuse for colour-combination.

Derain, as a Fauvist painter, already limited himself to a restrained scale of colour, relying chiefly on browns running from almost black to almost red, Poussin-blue, and grey. He was even then more adaptive than inventive—the conservative of the movement. But there is evidence of great wealth of thought and feeling in his reduction of visible form to its essentials which characterises this part of his production. An intermediate process of transformation, which gives the impression of a double artifice, seems to have taken place in his treatment of his subjects before he transfers to canvas their final aspect in his mind. Between Nature and painting they have been changed into formal images which appear to be invested with other physical properties than their originals. Thus his landscapes are like paintings of popular prints of landscape, his flower-pieces like paintings of artificial flowers, his figures like dolls or marionettes. But always he retains a sense of volume throughout this process of simplification by imagistic transference.

Utrillo was a Fauve in the literary and romantic suggestion that he brought to his work, though technically he was the most classical and traditional painter of the movement. There was nothing very revolutionary about his slightly simplified realism, and the whites, greys and greens of which he was a master from the first are not accentuated above fidelity. Yet their predominance in his work and his constant choice of scenes in which they figure most largely give his pictures an atmosphere all their own. Not only the appearance but the aura, of certain streets in Montmartre and at the back of Montmartre have been imperishably recorded by Utrillo, and in the sordidness and despair which his presentation of them so poignantly evokes, one may read a personal statement as clear as written autobiography. The enchantment of a lunar region is woven by exquisite harmonies of colour about a region of decaying stones, extenuate greenery and crapulous associations. Never has the Fauvist talent for translating intrinsic ugliness into terms of beauty been so triumphantly exercised.

There is a certain amount of Utrillo's lyricism in the work of Vlaminck, though he is for the most part content with a quickness of impression that hardly goes beyond a sketch. Roads in the hybrid district where suburb touches country, and little villages isolated on the great plain of La Beauce are his favourite subjects, but over them he throws a curious atmospheric intensity; he is especially a weather-painter, delighting to seize on the crisis of clouds. He conveys the feeling of snow, intense heat, and rain, with a few vigorous strokes and hastily defined partitions of colour. Though his work is only hurriedly selective and contains little formal composition, it is rhythmic and alive.

Sophistication, whether of method or emotion, stamps most of the Fauvist output. Its very simplicity was the result of complication, and intentional rather than spontaneous. The movement lacked its Primitive, but he was imported from without. Guillaume Apollinaire, an admirable poet, and, as an art critic, a vigorous propagandist of the new spirit in painting, discovered a retired *Douanier*, or customs-house officer, Henri Rousseau, whose Sunday holidays had long been devoted to the pursuit of art. Once a member of the French forces sent to Mexico in aid of Maximilian's tragic expedition, Rousseau had come back with a vivid recollection of the luxuriant shapes and colours of the tropical forest. These he carefully portrayed in canvases of a genuine naïveté both of imagination and execution. But he turned his attention also to scenes of contemporary life, in the portraiture of bourgeois groups and landscapes, of the outskirts of Paris. There is a distinct charm in the unforced fidelity of his work, with its absence of all technical trickery. The dream-pictures are strangely concrete, while on the other hand there is a curious fantasy in the unflinching effort at verisimilitude which marks his realism. With the means at his disposal, he faced squarely the problems of his art. His many excellences of clear pattern, and his power of perceiving this in unpromising externals, are so many individual conquests in expression. The Fauves eagerly co-opted this brave old man, who had hewn out his own pathway to beauty, into their group, and although dealers have produced a host of self-educated painters from the humbler walks of life, known, after his example, as "Sunday painters," they have never discovered a second Rousseau.

For all its seriousness of purpose as regards experiment and the invasion of new kingdoms of form and colour, Fauvism makes, in the solemn pages of art-history, an interval of gaiety. There was so much about it that was fresh and enthusiastic, so vivid a sense of new vistas opening-up and inviting joyous exploration. It developed in a sordid environment, but drew something exquisite from the sordidness; it was a movement of disorder, but before it died away, the disorder had brought new gifts to the treasure-house of tradition.

The best way to estimate the importance of its adherents is to note the ability with which they survived it. Yet it was Fauvism that endowed some of the most prominent leaders of the modern movement with self-realisation, and gave arms and experience to their later development.

Chapter Four: PICASSO THE INVENTOR

ONE of the most active of the Fauves, and certainly the most disconcerting, was Pablo Picasso, a young Spaniard whom the ever-increasing prestige of Paris had lured from Barcelona, to satisfy his eagerness to be in the centre of contemporary art-activity. How many, on his account, were afterwards to follow him thither from all parts of the world, seeking the same goal.

At the epoch of Fauvism he had already passed with astonishing rapidity through several phases, during which he had produced work of quality sufficient to consolidate a reputation. It seemed as though he had only to be in contact with a style in art that interested him, for him to produce an imitation of it. But there was something beyond the mere spirit of imitation in this. Picasso saw that the best way of understanding any particular process is by performing it oneself; and the proof that he was not content only with the aping of others' methods lies in the quickness with which they successively exhausted his interest. The old masters and, above all, his own country's El Greco, in turns incited him to this analytic, practical system of investigation. Among the moderns his experimental adaptability was exercised on the Impressionists, Toulouse-Lautrec, the fashionable Sargent and the democratic Steinlen—wherever there was something to learn, something to add to a prodigious storehouse of technique.

But soon enough he was moulding into coherence a manner of his own. His first personal expression, freed from the trammels of pastiche—one might almost say, his first non-laboratory painting—was a combination of racial influence, narrowed down into a formula of Spanish baroque, mingled with contemporary realism. But to this mixture he brought a welding element of style which was entirely individual.

The canvases of this period are mainly a series of figure-groups, which in form partake at once of the superficially pathetic implications of popular realistic illustration and the deeper tragic symbolism of Spanish religious sculpture. To the compounding of this recipe, however, Picasso added his own gifts. The emaciated anatomies, eloquent of poverty and starvation, are uniformly portrayed in different keys of blue, which gave to the painting of this time the name of the Blue Period, and of which *La Vie* is a fine example. The amount of expression which Picasso evoked from the use of this one colour was the first distinct manifestation of his genius. He handled it with such virtuosity, varying its tone from the light and diaphanous to the deepest possible shade, that there was no monotony in its employment. It speaks and does duty for other colours as well. Later, Picasso was to say, not altogether in jest, that if he found a tube of colour lacking from his paint-box in the course of a picture, he could equally well substitute another for it. The Blue Period is more than a hint at such prestidigitation. In appreciating the revolution in form that he was to effect in more recent stages of development, his wonderful talent as a colourist is not always sufficiently regarded.

To the Blue Period succeeded the Pink Period, exercised on much the same run of subject, but in a different colour-predominance. In spirit, the icy detachment of the blue gives way to a certain tenderness of attitude, while in design the Pink Period is more flowing, more versatile in gesture. Then came a series of paintings of mules and horses, in which, without establishing a White Period, that colour is largely employed. The main interest in these compositions, besides their curious dream-like property, lies in their remarkable facility of line, so rhythmic and uncramped as to approach the arabesque. At this stage of his achievement, Picasso had definitely asserted his originality as realist, colourist, and master of design ; but the assertion had been made, as it were, sectionally, as though at different times one pictorial element had interested him more than another. In the next phase, that of the circus pictures, these elements were to be blended, and from their blending the Picasso of to-day, the same in impulse although of many different manifestations, was to emerge.

In France the circus still keeps its supremacy in the domain of popular amusement. In Paris itself it has several permanent establishments, and Montmartre contains the delightful Cirque Medrano. There is, too, the *Fete Foraine*, which all the year round is in session in some part of the capital or its outskirts. Annually, at a given season, it stretches along the main thoroughfare of Montmartre and on to the outer boulevards, with its row of stalls, roundabouts and smaller circus-booths. Thus, a little way down the hill from the artist's studio, there awaited him a spectacle kaleidoscopic in its flare of lights, its motley tints, and its emotional admixture of humanity and artifice. It awoke echoes of the sturdy vagabond life of his native country, delighted him with the variety of its aspects, and appealed to his painter's enthusiasm.

The circus pictures were the turning-point of Picasso's career. To begin with, they are strongly realistic, with a considerable romantic, literary atmosphere. There is the same feeling for pathetic situation and the hardness of life's struggle which is evident in the Blue Period. The old Rigoletto theme of sorrow in tinsel, with tears behind the mask, is freely exhibited. They are mainly paintings of the life of acrobats behind the scenes. In their gaudy trappings, the bodies, though muscular, are ill-nourished ; the features droop with an unspeakable lassitude. But gradually the human sensibility pervading them gives way to a sensibility exclusively pictorial ; the tears are ignored in the artist's concentration on the mask ; the personality of the acrobat yields to the painter's problems offered by his uniform.

Through the series of circus pictures we see the æsthetic passion in Picasso gradually overwhelming his interest in humanity, as far as his painting is concerned. Henceforth, for years, literature is to be banished from his canvas. The acrobats become stylised figures of convention, developing gradually, by way of the lozenge-patterned costume in which he had begun almost exclusively to clothe them, into the protagonists of an up-to-date harlequinade of gesture. And his preoccupation with the lozenge pattern of Harlequin's livery was the first indication of Picasso's Cubism.

But his work had to undergo further modifications before Cubism was elaborated as a conscious form. Reminiscences of Watteau and engravings of the eighteenth-century *Commedia dell' Arte* helped to construct the ballet in pose and pattern, performed by lay-figures, which was Picasso's next phase. Then came Fauvism, with its crowd of new theories and release from old conventions. In Picasso's case it was his own convention that he set about breaking, to remould its successor from the fragments.

The period was one of such rapid innovation, and his own spirit as an æsthetic pioneer was so mobile, that the result is much easier to discern than the process. One perceives his work becoming more and more dynamic. He had successively gathered line, colour and formal relationship into it ; his compositions had become essentially rhythmic, but it was a static rhythm of continuity, rather than one of motion. The pattern, for all its intricacy, tended to become decorative and superficial ; a review primarily of externals. Then, within a short space of time, we find the impression of cubical content, of mass, greatly accentuated, and an addition of what may best be called simultaneity, to the picture—an attempt to portray at the same time, on the same canvas, different points of view of the same object. This was Picasso's particular contribution to Fauvism. Deserting the rigidity of line with which the harlequinade-convention had been built up, he painted what at first sight were heads with three noses ; or pictures of people seen sideways or from the back, on top of pictures of them seen from the front. It was as though the spectator were looking from all points of the compass at once. And mingled with this was a brutal sweep of line, and a reduction of the subject, whether figure or landscape, to its most rudimentary essentials. It was a crumbling of Picasso's decorative architecture into something huddled and barbaric, yet vibrant with a feverish excitement. It was the interregnum of metamorphosis from which, newly-formed, sprang Cubism.

The hectic ebullition of this phase was stimulated by the introduction of an influence which was for the Fauves what the Japanese colour-print had been to the Impressionists—the discovery of negro sculpture. Certainly, the revelation of negro sculpture was prodigiously fruitful in result, and Picasso was the first painter of the epoch to utilise it. The most trustworthy account of his first acquaintance with it is given by Max Jacob, his friend, and himself a distinguished poet, novelist and painter. Picasso, in the company of Jacob and Apollinaire, was dining with Matisse at his flat.

" Then, Matisse took up from a piece of furniture a statuette in dark wood and showed it to Picasso. It was the first example of negro sculpture. Picasso held it in his hand all the evening. The next morning, when I arrived at his studio, the floor was strewn with leaves of 'Ingres' drawing-paper. On every sheet was a large drawing, almost the same one: a woman's face with a single eye, a nose that was too long, joining with the mouth, a lock of hair on the shoulder.

" Cubism had come to birth.

" This same woman made her appearance again on canvas. Instead of one only, there were two or three. Then there was the *Demoiselle d'Avignon*, a picture as large as a wall."

In the course of the series of circus pictures, Picasso gradually abandoned the representation of emotion in favour of representation alone; then the representation narrowed into conventionalisation of appearances to suit a pictorial purpose. There remained, however, a fidelity to type, if not to individuals. Representation and pictorial purpose shared the canvas between them. After the evening with Matisse's statuette, the balance was destroyed. The dark wooden image, in common with the rest of its kind, with its triumphant assertion of form and mass, had convinced the painter that the expression of these properties, as beautiful in themselves, was more important than fidelity to, or associations with, visible and natural appearances. Pure pictorial expression, apart from representation, or with representation an utterly secondary and even accidental consideration, was his new aim. So long as to him there was beauty in the impression of line and volume which he gave, it mattered not whether his drawing of the woman's head had one eye or two. It mattered not, indeed, whether the drawing or painting carried a resemblance to any specific object either partially or at all, so long as itself it was an expression of beautiful form.

Just as abstract art is too general a term for it, so Cubism is too particular. But it is one of convenience, and is likely to remain, besides indicating a characteristic on which the school laid emphasis—the painter's analysis of his subject, whether pure pattern or more or less representation, into its component elements of mass, or cubical content; and conversely, his construction of his picture in such a way that an important condition of its appeal lies in the relationship of those elements.

If the discovery of negro sculpture caused Picasso's inception of Cubism, there were not wanting other influences for him to call into play in order to lend authority to his method. The investigation of Cézanne, whose work was conquering a posthumous popularity, showed that he, too, although eminently representational, had depended largely on a recession of planes and a sense of cubic pattern for his effect, and that his more important work could easily be reduced to abstract cubist composition. In fact, Cubism, whether conscious or not, could be traced as a basic part of their design with El Greco, Giotto, and the Byzantine workers in mosaic and fresco.

These masters were hailed as the ancestors of the movement by its adherents. Picasso was of course its leader. His impetuous zeal for experiment has not confined him within its limits, and there have been phases when his explorations have taken him along a very different course, but he has also frequently returned to it, bringing a new subtlety, a new charm. The contribution of negro art was a liberating one, freeing him from the trammels of fidelity to visible appearances, bringing a new dimension to his means of expression. But its influence was not long-lasting, and the first cubist epoch in which he moved with freedom in a realm of imagery definitely his own took the form of a series of sublimated still-lifes. Objects seem always to have attracted Picasso towards the release of what was more individual in his painter's temperament, and to have awakened fewer echoes in him. A fragment from the period of the harlequinades, and perhaps a memory of Spain, led him to a stage of design evolved from the shape of guitars, presenting strange complexities of perspective, whose lines take on the arabesque formation of notes of music, and in which the variety of colour is suggested by infinite gradations of brown and grey. Or sometimes, instead of the guitar, the picture would be an abstract fantasy vaguely based on such still-life subjects as a newspaper, a glass and a carafe, suddenly arrested at its furthest point of departure from representation by the presence in a corner of a piece of imitative miniature-painting—perhaps a fruit, or an imitative copy of some other picture. Or again, landscapes and figures would be dissolved and re-formed into an intricate pattern of basic geometric shapes which luxuriate in richness of volume.

In a later phase, the third-dimensional element is abandoned in favour of the purely decorative surface qualities of these geometric figures. Afterwards, still remaining superficial, but founded on more associations with actuality, came a series of tables covered with stuffs falling in a wilderness of cylindrical folds and supporting a mass of heterogeneous " properties "—scrolls, birdcages, busts, dishes of fruit—all woven into a sternly-controlled austerity of design, yet bristling with pictorial incident. Then, as in the splendid *Le Tapis Rouge*, this arrangement took on cubical content and was infused with a glowing wealth of various colour. This period was followed by exercises merely in black, flowing line against a neutral background, and strange contrivances in form, like abstractions of dentition, or horses' skulls, which were studies in the enclosure of space. For Picasso is not only the inventor of a pictorial treatment of the shapes of natural appearances; he is an inventor of shape itself. To design, merely as design, he has brought new strength by giving it new foundations; for art he has conquered a fresh world of wonder and excitement by insisting on the painter's right to create his own form.

Yet by his versatility and the thoroughness of his exploration, he has himself exhausted the possibilities of his discovery. Outside Picasso there is very little Cubism that is not an imitation of his. Braque, keeping for the most part to a restrained scale of greens and greys, has applied the Cubist analysis into third-dimensional elements to statuesque, sibylline female figures, and multiplied delightful still-life panels of fruit and flowers. There is a sameness verging on monotony in a collection of his work, which is not relieved by his never departing really far from representation; although such variation as he evolves from a deliberate paucity of theme compels admiration. The pictures are more comprehensive singly than in numbers; their discipline and grasp of pattern can then be appreciated better. As Picasso is the romantic, so Braque is the classic of the movement.

Juan Gris is as restrained as Braque, with brown as a predominant key of colour, and employing greater abstraction within his particular limits of design. Like Braque, he devoted himself to the cultivation of one of Picasso's transient epochs, the two-dimensional geometric pattern. His work is hardly more than a footnote to painting, a series of enlarged vignettes, which are an up-to-date equivalent of the eighteenth-century arms trophies so often used for chapter-endings of books. But they have a delicate lyrical quality, and are valuable to the theorist of the movement in showing that associational representation is not necessary to obtain something more than intellectual satisfaction from it, and that Cubism, even without Picasso's direct, compelling magic, is capable of evoking a mood.

Fernand Leger, in his scenes of contemporary life and his landscapes, effects a clever compromise between his subjects' own pictorial qualities and the Cubist abstraction of pattern to which they could be reduced. But many other practitioners of the method have brought to it little more than a technical facility and a talent for adaptation. They have not out-distanced Picasso in discovery, or left the mark of an independent personality in the new realm which he has traversed. They have been content merely with following in the wake of a vogue, and although their work bears signatures, it is actually anonymous, a kind of standardised mass-production.

Although French Cubism was wholly an æsthetic movement, it has had its repercussion outside pure art. In the opportunities for art to be applied to the decoration of life, apart from the picture and the statue, it has been freely introduced. Architecture, interior decoration, stage setting, and ornament, have all been influenced by it, while a number of Cubist painters have turned their attention to the design of patterned fabrics, to which it has proved extremely appropriate.

It has cleared painting of much irrelevant literature, and weeded away survivals of traditionalism which no longer served any vital purpose. Its value in widening the scope of art and in stimulating a continuity of development has been incalculable. Yet on its own merits apart from being the expression of the genius who invented and perfected it, it is narrow and sectional as a movement. Its lack of contact with human life and Nature, when carried to any great extent along its lines of logical development, prevents its expansion beyond ornament and the display of technical ingenuity. In itself it is a cul-de-sac, but its early battles were a healthy excitement, and its influence, under other forms, is not extinct.

Chapter Five: FUTURISM

THE application of Cubism and its transformation from a purely æsthetic purpose, complete in itself, towards other channels, was most accentuated in Italy. There it gave birth to the movement known as Futurism, whose consequences have been so considerable that they justify a momentary desertion of the Parisian scene.

A group of Italian painters, sculptors, writers and musicians, under the leadership of the poet Marinetti, had for some time been dissatisfied with their native land ranking as little more than a museum-country among the nations. They found that their own careers were thwarted by a dead weight of tradition, which stifled attempts at original expression. Even the energetic concentration of the national spirit in the literature of their most talented contemporary, D'Annunzio, had led to little more than a revival—vivid and impetuous, but still only a revival—of obsolete forms. Alert to the new developments of art in Paris, they found in Cubism, both in spirit and manifestation, something that they might adapt to their own need of release.

It encouraged them to voice, in a series of fiery manifestos, the doctrine of Futurism, and it is possible that these vociferous, vitriolic statements of their aims were of greater importance than the actual works of art in which they were carried out. Unlike the Cubists, they demanded that the æsthetic technique, which they borrowed directly from the Parisian movement, should be carried into life, instead of remaining simply an artistic expression. They made it the rallying-point of an attitude that was applicable also to philosophy, politics and behaviour. A turn was given it that transformed it, in its implications, into a practical gospel of energy and modernity.

Italy was to be freed from its past. Museums and art galleries filled with the work of the old masters were to be abolished, or at any rate closed. Instead, what was dynamic in contemporary existence should be exalted. The game of football, which just then was beginning to make some headway in the country, was chosen as an excellent stimulus to the genuine modern spirit. But, above all, the machine was glorified.

Curiously enough, French Cubism, which was essentially a product of the studios, and, in original conscious intention a movement of refinement rather than expansion, while naturally uninterested in machinery on its own account, had shown hardly any appreciation of machine-forms as a subject. Yet these forms were peculiarly adapted to Cubist treatment. The Futurist School seized on them eagerly, with the then imperfect aeroplane as their best manifestation. It is, indeed, to the credit of Futurism that it conquered the strange timidity of art in the face of mechanics, and triumphantly carried the machine into the field of artistic expression.

The Futurist painters, it must be confessed, were not very much more than skilful adaptors of the earliest analytic phase of Cubism. The novelty which they brought to it lay mainly in the choice of subject. Having chosen their scenes from actuality, or conceived them in the imagination from the daily spectacle of life, they proceeded to split them, though keeping a basis of representation, into their component elements of primary volume-pattern. In colour they used uniformly the browns and greys of Picasso's first guitars. Enthusiasm of spirit and the conscientious accomplishment of a laborious process must be granted them.

But it is chiefly owing to what was good in Futurism that Futurism itself is at the present time so out of date. Essentially an adaptation, it had no æsthetic basis of its own; it is marginalia to marginalia. The adaptations that it gave rise to, however, though outside the achievements of art, are pursuing a vigorous career. Stripped of its bombast, and though its own attempt at its object was not very successful pictorially, it gave, as we have seen, an "art-prestige" to machinery. Through it, Cubism was expanded by being made applicable, in modified form, to a greater variety of subject. It was popularised, stripped of a good deal of its ultimate nullity, and, through the variations upon Futurism, turned back towards representation. And to representation, at the hands of many artists, it now gives an agreeable, minor accent of conventionalised style.

It is by its adaptation to advertisement, however, that Futurism, greatly diluted, now survives. By its function of vulgarisation, in the good sense of the word, it established a liaison between what was vital in contemporary art-movements and the advertiser's pictorial appeal. In the popular portrayal of machinery, or processes of industry, and in a rough-and-ready imaginative rendering of them, with the emphasis necessary to advertisement, a kind of rudimentary Futurism now plays an important part. There is no reason why this commercial use of design, which makes art democratic by taking it into the streets, should not, on its broader lines and in some of its aspects, be a satisfaction in form and colour, and related to more definitely æsthetic contemporary artistic expression. Very considerable progress in this direction has, indeed, been made already; and it ought not to be forgotten that Futurism, by insisting that industrial life and mechanisation was a fit theme for art, put art in the service of industry as well. Only good can come to both of them by the relationship.

Chapter Six: THE FREEDOM OF DESIGN

ALTHOUGH Cubism was an expansion of artistic method, it was, in its orthodox canons, self-limited. It did not include a large section of painting activity which went on simultaneously with it. Picasso, while he was still working out its possibilities, took holidays from his own invention, experimenting along his old Fauvist lines. Sometimes this took the form of definite representation very near to realism, with a happy elasticity of line, but with the intentional distortion of a particular feature, or an accentuation of the sense of mass, without any reference to its Cubist rendering. Whether within or outside Cubism, he has never stopped testing new means of formal expression, and, since he changes as much as he continues, and preserves a tireless curiosity, more surprises are yet to be expected from him than from any of his contemporaries.

His fellow Fauves, to all appearances, sowed their pictorial wild oats during that hectic epoch. Cubism left them untouched, and a strengthening of what was traditional in their talent has become noticeable with the passage of time. But the discovery of negro sculpture and the example of Cubism, without its practice, made their approach to tradition a very different matter from what it would otherwise have been. They remained impenitent independents, making a catholic choice of their points of adherence, and jealously guarding a freedom that Fauvism had won. With the exception of the Cubists, French painting was, for once, not running in schools.

They continued to stick to the broad basis of representation, but they affirmed their right to a personal manner in carrying it out, to a deformation of reality when it suited their interpretation of it. If they did not go so far as the invention of new form, at any rate in the rendering of existing visible form they insisted on exercising their individuality. In this, without retrogression or violent change, they followed a logical progress in developing, which the Great War interrupted, but did not break.

The end of the cataclysm brought a change in the conditions under which French painters worked. With peace had come the appearance of prosperity; a spirit of happy relaxation was in the air. Art, along with other luxury products, profited from the care-free spending that was one of the symbols of victory. There was, too, a genuine demand for it. After four years of terrible reality there was comfort in turning towards a vision of life presented by the artificers of beauty.

Paris became to young artists from other countries something of what London had been to Dick Whittington. Why should it not be for them a region of promise admirably fulfilled, as it had been for Picasso? In no other capital could he have gained the same hearing, and carried off the same palm. The emigrants of art swarmed across Europe and across the ocean to the City of Light. To some it was to award the prize of success; it did not too brusquely shatter the others' illusions.

Montmartre had ceased to be the painters' quarter, chiefly on account of economic reasons. Both war and victory had put a premium on pleasure. Cabarets and *boîtes de nuit*, where champagne and evening dress were obligatory, had sprung up where once were cafés and little wine-shops offering shelter to those pressed by the need of æsthetic discussion. The seeker and the purveyor of pleasure crowded out the writer and artist; there was less good-fellowship between the two clans. A few incorrigible Montmartrois stayed where they were; but those who were less firmly established trekked through the city and over the river to the district of Montparnasse, where they were joined by the newcomers from abroad.

It was an appropriate neighbourhood, for it bordered on the University region of the Sorbonne and the Boulevard Saint-Michel, and painting, for the Cubists, had developed almost into a branch of science. For its other practitioners, too, it had become a much more scholarly affair than it was in the days of Fauvism. Experiments were made less light-heartedly, and more in the spirit of serious research. Tradition and the history of art were more intensely explored, and for that purpose libraries were more easily at hand than was the case with Montmartre. It was no longer the exception for a painter to be well-read and deeply versed in the accomplishment of his predecessors both inside and outside Europe. The old Bohemian type, for whose education outside the studios an occasional visit to the Italians in the Louvre had sufficed, was dying out. And as painting, though centred in Paris, grew more cosmopolitan, the nearness of another cosmopolitan quarter, the students' domain, made Montparnasse an agreeable place of sojourn for the young artist arriving from abroad.

It had many attractions of its own. On one side the Luxembourg Gardens bounded it, with their lake and majestic avenues. And as it possessed already its life as a popular quarter, it had its proper share of entertainments and cafés, which were not yet expensively exclusive, like those of Montmartre. There was room for the foundation and expansion of an artist's colony. They settled down accordingly at the corner of the Boulevard Montparnasse and the Boulevard Raspeil. As the poets had their café nearby at the *Closerie des Lilas*, and the senior "arrived" painters theirs, half-way down towards the river at *Les Deux Magots* in the Boulevard Saint-Germain, so the young artists elected for their places of assembly the two cafés on opposite sides of the corner mentioned, the

Café de la Rotonde and the *Café du Dôme*. They were hardly ever in both at the same time; one would be full while the other was empty. At the impulse of incalculable caprice they flitted, like departing swallows, in a body, from one to the other.

The history of Montparnasse, as an artist's quarter, is very like that of Montmartre. There was the same nucleus of serious workers and the larger flock of dilettantes; the struggle for existence held the same tragedy and comedy. The cosmopolitanism, however, was distinctly a difference, and it may be remarked that sometimes the two cafés contained also a sprinkling of Russian and Near Eastern political refugees, of whom M. Trotsky was for long a prominent member. This contact was not without making its contribution to the painting of Montparnasse; it did something towards giving it its air of actuality, of preventing it from lagging behind other movements of the spirit and tending to lapse into the production of a closed, self-centred corporation. Though since Fauvism, painting, in its general spirit, no longer waited to take its cue from literature, but gave suggestions to the other arts, or at least had a more reciprocal relation with them.

The first prominent painter of Montparnasse, though the prominence was not awarded until after his early death, was Modigliani. This young Italian was more directly influenced by negro sculpture than any other painter of importance, with the exception of Picasso. And with Picasso its effect was that of a spring-movement, bringing into play workings beyond itself, providing the sudden though decisive hint which started his activity in more remote directions. But with Modigliani, in the surprising amount of work he managed to achieve, the negro influence possesses it in its entirety. Yet though it was so strong an influence, Modigliani met it on equal terms, thoroughly mastered its mechanism, turned it inside out, and made it yield to his purpose. He did not so much adapt it as translate it. Disregarding its encouragement to construction in volume, as far as painting was concerned, for he made several pieces of sculpture obviously derived from it, he employed only its two-dimensional surface properties, making use of it merely for simplification of line. He drew from it the essentials of his style in draughtsmanship, and, since he confined himself to portraiture, imprinted its linear characteristics on his sitters. Eyes are reduced to a convention of round or oval, noses elongated and thinned, lips contracted, while as a whole the figure at once joins the category either of etiolation or expansion. There is no middle, normal course; the slightest excess of balance one way or the other is deformed into its particular alternative, just as negro sculpture is either squat and bulky, or extenuated and reed-like. Yet within this intentionally rudimentary convention, Modigliani amazingly conveys likeness, which is saved from caricature by the delicate grace of his lengthened forms, the rich sense of healthy flesh and abundance of his expanded ones. To this sublimation of his design is joined a lustrous clarity of colour. There are no half-tones; the colour, evenly laid on, is allowed its full force of expression. This enhances the subtle lucidity of his effect, and gives force to the exquisitely attenuated line. The whole figure, according as it falls into one of the two classes, has the equivalent quality in painting of a Gothic or Romanesque arch. And his portraits, confined to a small range of types—Montparnasse friends, servants from the country, and nudes—charmingly self-conscious as they are, with a kind of intellectual naïveté, have the same authority of statement as fine architecture.

Modigliani is an extreme though successful instance of the artist's exercise of his newly-acknowledged right of deformation upon appearances. But it must be remembered that this deformation was practised for the ends of painting alone, for the perfection of the artist's expression through the picture of his conception of beauty in form. It was analytic reconstruction in terms of vision and for the sake of vision, without any implications of drama and literature. The spectator might transfer its effect in his mind to other arts, it might arouse in him conceptions of poetry, comedy or tragedy. It might bring with it, in its result, a sense of the contemporaneous; but itself, in its own assertion, it was independent of all but painting, as painting.

For the art was nearing a purity of individual expression, which it had not known before the modern movement began. It had started to be self-sufficing and to enjoy a completeness of existence from the following-out of its own laws. The painter's attitude was rapidly getting farther from that of the dramatist or descriptive writer, and approaching the musician's, or the mathematician's. And thus, to claim consideration, the painter had to bring technical interest and originality to his subject, which on its own account was rapidly decreasing in the importance of its contribution to the picture; his justification as an artist depended on the value of his expression in technique.

Innovation in this respect was no longer looked on askance, as in the days of the Impressionists and Post-Impressionists; instead, it was a proof that the artist, whether to a lesser or a large degree, had a statement to make which would lift his work from the rut of imitation. The prominent Fauves of pre-war days had set an example to be followed in this direction. Something of the light-heartedness, which had occasionally verged upon bravado, was gone from their work; but eccentricity was not the kind of innovation which the new epoch demanded—nothing becomes monotonous so soon. The post-war generation wanted a novelty that should be serious, that should stand the test of time and be the richer for continued practice. The surviving

Fauves had shed what was once momentarily exciting in their work, and such part of its novelty as was incapable of endurance. But the maturer gifts which they revealed more than justified the brave adventures of their youth.

Matisse no longer left the spectator to fill in mentally the blank spaces of his design. He filled them in himself, so that time should not be wasted over them, and with a facility of draughtsmanship that could be as firm and subtle as he wanted, but that he preferred not to elaborate. For as soon as it had become simply divisional in function, that is to say, as soon as it performed the duty of bounding space, he had no more need for it in the picture. All that he sought was an effect of colour and light, both exhibited in their most limpid quality. The spatial relationship, equally with the line, is subordinated to them; mass, though he could be a master of it when he would, is unimportant; he adopted representation because, for his aims, he had no need to go beyond it. He painted cliffs fronting the sea, fish, modish women, and odalisques couched in a luxury of tapestries and patterned stuffs. But these forms, indicated with varying degrees of fidelity from realism to vague suggestion, are only an excuse for the pure subjectivity of his colour-harmony. There, the whole gamut of tints is employed with dazzling coruscation. Such painting is remote from time and place; it is expression in its most clarified essence.

Although Derain has become deliberately reactionary in manner, he has shown himself, among his contemporaries, the most nearly approaching to Picasso in versatility. But his experiments have been towards the past, rather than forward-reaching. His Fauvist puppetry yielded before a realism which was practised, however, on a subject of fantasy. On his own account he constructed a harlequinade. But his adaptation of the figures of eternal comedy is altogether a matter-of-fact affair; they are plainly studio-models at the service of a costume-painter. For though as a Fauve he reduced its dimensions, and though as a painter of harlequinade he made it wear a disguise, Derain cannot escape from his inborn fidelity to appearances. In modern French painting he is the equivalent of Chardin, as Matisse is of Watteau. The one is reason, the other instinct; and each is a supreme example of two characteristic types of the French spirit. In the end, Derain has yielded to his realism, but he has tempered it with an admirable faculty for selection, and infused it with the spirit of classic tradition. In this he has shown a boldness which has won him from enthusiasts of modernity, whose endeavour has outrun their good intentions, the epithet of "museum-painter." Yet if, in these later days, he has often entered the museums, he has left them again in order to breathe in the sense of actuality, that has been but fortified by the visit. He has not reverted to a tradition that is outworn, but has continued tradition and injected the flame of contemporary life into it. There is a force of reference in his work, but a fine dignity of reserve keeps it in the background, whence it lends authority to Derain's own conservative yet virile style. And this style he has exercised upon still-lifes where, from a limited range of theme and scale of colour, he provides a wealth of pictorial incidents ; on portraits of women in which he has unashamedly invited the beauty of the sitters to collaborate on equal terms with his beauty of treatment, and which are distinguished by notable plastic qualities ; and on Provençal landscapes and woodland scenes where fidelity to the scene wedded to power of selection diffuses over the canvas a charm like that of an early Corot.

Utrillo, who even as a Fauve did not depart far from tradition, has changed less than the other painters of that period. Some of his work shows traces of too mechanical a production ; but in the better specimens the curious enchantment of his colour, in which a lunar milkiness increasingly gains ground, is emphasised at the expense of form. *Le Lapin Agile* shows him in one of his alerter moods, before an existence too ardently Bohemian had made a legend of his personality, but sadly enfeebled his expression. It is interesting too—and with Utrillo subject-qualities can be taken into account—as a picture of what was once a famous rendezvous of the Montmartre group of artists and writers. Of Vlaminck, one need only say that his work has not changed, but has increased immeasurably in depth of feeling. He, too, has sought reinforcement from tradition, and the later canvases contain an echo of Constable, without losing any of the old rhythmic impetuosity.

Dufy, one of the younger Fauves, whose work did not reach maturity until after the war, is the painter now nearest to the spirit of that movement. In his arabesque design, delight in colour, and flowing two-dimensional decoration, he inevitably reminds one of the earlier Matisse ; though, in his swift notations of it, he has elaborated a kind of stenographic realism. His pictures of cities and southern harbours sparkle gaily in their combination of clear and varied colour and vivid line ; his is essentially happy painting.

The painters mentioned in this chapter were the doyens of post-war accomplishment, so far as the modern movement is concerned, with the exception of the Cubists. By their refusal to be involved in that group, which, despite the deep imprint it has made on twentieth-century painting, has had a nullifying effect on all its whole-hearted practitioners but Picasso, they rescued their art from a risk of detachment from human significance, and of losing much vitality and scope in its expression.

Chapter Seven: REVALUATIONS

THE modern movement is a development of the art of the past. The changes it has brought about have arisen from dissatisfaction with academic officialism, which tried to impose a particular tradition on artists who desired independence. They did not revolt against tradition as a whole, but they refused to model their work on a section of it which they considered exhausted as a force of contemporary suggestion. A painter who has received no help from the study of his predecessors, immediate or farther back, has for centuries been an almost impossible phenomenon. The Impressionists protested against help that was tyranny disguised, but they sought it at other points of contact with the long line of tradition, thus effecting again the revaluation that accompanies every stage of artistic evolution. In place of the prescribed examplers of *chiaroscuro* and *beau idéal*, they sought guidance from Velazquez and Goya, and, nearer their own day, Delacroix. Of their contemporaries, they opposed Courbet, with his bold sense of mass, to the *pompiers* of the Salon.

The Post-Impressionists widened the field of influence by introducing the exotic element, finding authority for their technical departures in Japanese colour-prints and the sculpture and totem-forms of Polynesia. This blow to the exclusiveness of the European tradition in European art has had an effect that still continues. Besides these conscious adaptations, art-historians have found a relation between past epochs of European tradition and the Post-Impressionists, especially in the case of Cézanne. There is a similar use of planes to his, and a geometric pattern, in the Byzantines, Giotto and El Greco, and the study of these artists has been revived by his followers.

Then came the contact with negro sculpture, so sharply affecting Picasso and Modigliani, while further influences on Picasso's non-cubist periods are Ingres and the brothers Le Nain. Derain has painted a series of heads which are related to Egyptian portraiture, and Matisse has received much suggestion from Persian design. Nowadays, indeed, a variety of adaptation from world-wide tradition is a common feature of the galleries. It is an impediment instead of an aid unless its employers subjugate it to answering a genuine purpose in their own creation. Yet this intensive revaluation of the past has brought with it the excitement of discovery and an impulse to new vitality.

Among the ancestors of the modern movement whose imprint has been most marked on its later generations, Cézanne comes first. Apart from the Cubists, a large portion of French painting since the beginning of the century has been dominated by him. This method fitted with fatal ease into a recipe, and a lamentable number of pseudo-Cézannes, whose work never attained greater merit than pastiche, acquired a trick of receding planes and a geometric pattern-analysis of appearances. But while seizing on these characteristics, they unhappily ignored, or were incapable of approaching, Cézanne's genius as a colourist. Landscapes, portraits, figures grouped or isolated, nudes, still-lifes—the whole range was run over in a myriad of canvases, all more or less neatly partitioned off into cubes, cones, spheres and cylinders, or, with those of weaker accomplishment, into squares, triangles, circles and rectangles. Beyond a superficial dexterity there was little to merit attention in such combinations of jig-saw puzzles and illustrations to Euclid. They betokened no individuality of expression, and the colour-timidity of their artificers rarely adventured beyond a monotonous repetition of muddy-greens, browns and greys. Dinginess of colour cried clumsiness of form. Ultimately, as agglomerated cowardice swells into the brutish truculence of the mob, these Cézannicules exalted the very meanness and negation of their achievement into a quality, preferring a definite association of dreariness in their subject to one of interest, yet not translating it into any beauty of expression of their own. The subject, with incompetent emphasis, was left displaying its inherent lack of grace, twisted into pointless distortion, and smeared with a degradation of tint. Such inverted homage was a corruption of Cézanne's magnificent example, and its wearisome area stretches across the history of modern painting like the Slough of Despond.

An attention of humility to the lessons of the master of Aix, and their absorption in a real expression of individuality, can have nothing but a salutary effect. It is a blatancy of imitation that is disastrous. Such painters at Othon Friesz, with his finely-composed groups in a setting of rocky woodland scenery ; Kisling, with the graceful restraint of his portraiture and the intellectual discipline of his sun-bathed landscapes ; and Dufresne, with the profusion of his oriental fantasies and still-lifes, are good types of those artists who have thoroughly searched into the principles of Cézanne's painting, but have not allowed them more than a temperate share of what remains a personal achievement.

The reaction from excessive imitation of Cézanne led many painters back to Corot's early landscapes and his portraiture, though not to the Corot of the nymphs and synthetic trees. There was a reservoir of force and inspiration in his union of instinct and intellect, and his fidelity to appearances, yet without slavish detail. His reticence of statement, clarity of colour, logical construction, and the even distribution of interest over the whole of the canvas were an encouragement to modern adherents to selective representation upon classic lines. The harbours, stations and bridges of Marquet, in their restrained colour-scale; the draped figures and nudes of Marchand; and Pequin's grave, luminous still-lifes, are representative of this calm and lucid "Right-Wing" painting.

Renoir is another painter upon whom attention has been turned with much greater eagerness since the decline of Cézanne's empire. He may almost be said to have enjoyed two existences in art, first as an Impressionist, and then as a Post-Post-Impressionist. Living from 1841 to 1919, he accomplished work of more importance in the twentieth than in the nineteenth century. His earlier work is full of charm, but the painting of the later period has a tangibility beside which it is hardly more than a shadow of delightful hue. He still used Impressionist processes, dividing his colour, enveloping his subject in atmosphere, and giving it vibration, though these means were now directed to concentration and construction. The result was no longer an "impression," in the sense of something delicate and evanescent. Its effect of motion was one of strength rather than time, continuously dynamic instead of instantaneous. The fleeting vision was replaced by a conception of permanence. These later paintings are distinguished by their sense of volume, which attains a primæval, monumental quality carrying the mind back to the abundance and robust grace of a Golden Age. Without distortion or pattern-emphasis, they show the delighted welcome Renoir gave to vivid colour and alluring form, his unabashed rendering of visible beauty in the intensest expression he could find for it.

The tendency to lyrical realism, which Renoir heightened to an epic pitch and invested with a glowing majesty, is evident in a humbler form in the work of Vuillard and Bonnard, the leaders of the Intimist School. It accounts for the appreciation which they are receiving at the present day, though by their methods and the date of their chief accomplishment, they were the immediate successors to the Impressionists. Their outline, however, is more clearly defined; while in the interiors which have given their particular kind of painting its name, they approach the formation of a definite later French *genre*. Their design is free and rapid; their composition has an air of easy fortuity whose effect is enhanced by the gem-like irradiation of their colour. Both in design and colour, Vuillard is the graver and more concentrated. His faithful realism is denied the romanticism in which Bonnard sometimes indulges. But in technique and subject—*bourgeois* interiors and Parisian street scenes—there is an identity of aim that places them on an equal level of prominence. Their lithography, which possesses the same exquisite, sensitive craftsmanship as their painting, is an important part of their production.

These older painters of the modern movement, with whom Rouault should also be included, and Corot from the past of tradition, are exercising considerable influence on the younger generation now that the divagation of Cubism in its pure form is reaching the end of its course. There is at present no outstanding tendency or school; it is a period of fusion, during which the spirit of revolution that has prevailed for the last half-century is gradually being absorbed in the most recent projection of tradition. The race is to the individual rather than the group; and the School of Paris is a collection of independent personalities united by locality rather than artistic affinity.

They are painters who have been drawn to the city from outside France, coming to it as to the world's acknowledged art-centre, and sure that somewhere amid its kaleidoscopic cosmopolitanism they would not feel on alien soil. From the point of view of numbers, they compose a school of formidable dimension, but only a few exceptionally gifted individuals have emerged from its collective anonymity. Pascin, a naturalised American from the Balkans, who committed suicide in 1930, was an instinctive painter. He combined an expressive suavity of technique with a gift of observation, half-witty and half sentimental, turned upon the less reputable features of the city's pleasure-organisation. There is a perverse prettiness about his nudes and figure-studies, but his deft handling of pigment, sure line and subtle colour are disciplined into a cohesion that attains pictorial harmony and is an expression in terms of painting that is of more importance than the implicit literature of the subject. Soutine, a Russian, is saved from being only a humourist-illustrator, as is Pascin from being no more than the illustrator of low gallantry, by his superiority in technique and the quality of his *matière*. These are exhibited in his pictures of poultry and joints of meat, which are of an impressive virtuosity; but the humour is apparent in the richly-coloured portraits, mostly of *bourgeois* and *employés*, which owe something to Modigliani in their attenuation of figure and are spiced with caricature. Chagall, another Russian, has a charming sense of colour, contained loosely in very free design. He is a poet of painting, with a child-like simplicity in his rendering of flowers, peasant scenes and dreams.

The dream-element of Chagall's work connects him also with Surrealism, a school more precise in definition on its literary than its pictorial side. With its researches into human conduct and emotion it combines the science of psychology with art, in which it advocates the expression of the sub-conscious freed as much as possible from intellectual control. In painting it forms a convenient label—which its sterner adherents would like to see less freely attached—for the large number of young artists who are returning to subject-interest, to literature and imagination. Signs of this tendency have been in evidence for some time. Besides Chagall, it was apparent in the tempered Cubism of Lurçat, with his solitary figures islanded in queer fenced enclosures amid a menace of sea and storm. Pierre Roy, another of its precursors, paints meticulous still-lifes as well as imaginative castles and interiors, and an almost exaggerated scrupulousness of draughtsmanship is a surrealist characteristic. Chirico, a leader of the movement, presents a strange world of white streets and broken marble columns, peopled by draped figures with rudimentary oval heads, and horses. Max Ernst is a poet-painter of imaginary islands, and Salvator Dali of mountain-rimmed landscapes variegated by minute cities and human figures, against which are juxtaposed larger detailed paintings of mechanical still-lifes or invented shapes in relation to each other but independent of the other contents of the canvas. Miro and Tanguy assemble heterogeneous miniatures, between which there is a vague or sub-conscious thought connection, in the same picture. Eugène Berman paints tragic fantasies of ruined cities, ports and wind-worn rocks.

Many of the painters mentioned in this chapter have yet to reach an achievement of permanent value, but they represent the liveliness in different sections of painting at the present day which has been caused by revaluations both in tradition and aesthetic purpose. The period of technical experiment seems now at an end, after much revolutionary achievement with which the painting of the future must be irrevocably tinged. Outside the realm of painting it has also left its stamp, whether by its abstract pattern-forms or its examples of deflection from realistic verisimilitude.

In this respect it has encouraged the *rapprochement* of art and industry, by widening the scope of applied art, heightening the pictorial quality of advertisement, and adding a variety to the common spectacle of life outside the walls of galleries. The influence of the modern movement on architecture, interior decoration and stage settings, of which a notable instance was the liaison between painters and the Russian ballet, has also been considerable, tending always to an economy of means to produce effect, and the sweeping away of a great deal of extraneous ornamentation.

By its desertion of the old academicism, painting has at all points been closely linked with other manifestations of the human spirit to a greater extent than was the case with the Impressionists' predecessors. This relationship has been more implicit than obvious ; but the concentration of the main currents of modern painting in Paris would make it not difficult to trace in its development a parallel with contemporary changes in the attitude of that city towards other aspects of life, such as internationalism, or the popularity of *le jazz*, *le dancing* and *le sport* which is an evidence of it. The tokens of a return to imagination and the picturesque are yet another manifestation of art as Proteus-Apollo, seeking, since the modern liberation, a still wider scope of expression, with the same invincible vitality. For while remaining independent in its own aesthetics, in itself neither a social nor a political activity, it is yet a reading of life, and brings to life its gift of tonic beauty that is an abiding fortification against despair.

Plate I

CEZANNE: Mont St. Victoire

Reproduced by courtesy of the Home House Trustees through the Courtauld Institute of Art

Paul Cézanne (1839-1906)

Cézanne was born at Aix, the son of a banker, and gave up the study of law to enter the Aix Museum Art School and later the Free Swiss Academy in Paris. Most of the later part of his life was passed at Aix.

" He painted essential shapes, bringing out relations of mass or volume, of approaching or receding planes of space, instead of contenting himself with surface and outline and approximate indications of distance and measurement. If what he was painting differed in some points of outward form from the authoritative form which he saw within it, then those divergences were irrelevant for him, and sacrificed. Within the picture there must be nothing that did not contribute to the unity imposed. He asserted the right of painting over Nature, for the ends of painting alone. Banishing all other intrusive, extraneous arts, he revolutionised the attitude of his own to the world before it."

" The region of Aix sprang into exquisite new being under his creation, radiant in colour through the variations of the Provençal year. He painted nude groups of a majestic simplicity, before which the pseudo-nymphs of the official schools withered into outworn conventionalism; in the portraits of himself and the folk about him he illuminated a homely beauty with the enthusiasm of a science unknown before. And in his studies of flowers and fruit he instilled a vibrant life of form into what had become an exercise in virtuosity. Working unencouraged and alone, he was an ascetic with gifts of abundance."

P. Cezanne

Plate 2

VAN GOGH: Chair

Reproduced by courtesy of the National Gallery, Millbank

Vincent Van Gogh (1853-1890)

Born at Zundert in North Brabant, Van Gogh was the son of a pastor with a large family. Teaching, art-dealing and preaching occupied him in turn until he found his true expression in painting. After a stormy career he shot himself.

" The glorification of the visible world through his gift of painting, by illustrating the beauty of form and colour, might be salvation to himself and the spring of thanksgiving to his fellows. He came to the conclusion that it was unnecessary for his pictures to bear a moral implication, like those of Millet, whom he had spent some time in imitating."

" That Van Gogh was a religious painter, that he attached to his painting a significance for himself more great than merely the production of a work of art, does not invalidate an æsthetic judgment on it, but it helps an understanding of its passionate emphasis. Once he was in full possession of his technique, he infused into it an ardour that was often excessive, though never empty or rhetorical. There are landscapes where Nature writhes in a cataclysm, portraits and still-lifes distorted with the force of their expression. Yet even in his excesses he displays so profound a delight in natural form, and seizes with such ardour the sudden revelations of colour which the visible world presented to him, that his pictorial statement always imposes the conviction from which it sprang."

Vincent

Plate 3

SEURAT: Le Pont de Courbevoie

Reproduced by courtesy of
The Connoisseur *and of the Courtauld Institute of Art*

Georges Seurat (1859-1892)

Seurat was born in Paris, and spent four years at the Ecole des Beaux Arts.

"*His figures flicker into being; they do not stand already placed before the spectator as entities independent of each other and their surroundings; the individual features of his landscapes stand out only gradually from the palpitating mirage in which they are interwoven. But the sense of motion or vibration, though at a slower pace than actuality, is complete; and the suave panellings of colour, lighted and suffused with points, like corpuscles, of a more vivid tint in the same key, attain a pictorial cohesion of great charm in spite of the atomic method by which they are produced.*

Seurat was a Parisian of the Parisians, and delighted to portray those amusements of the capital which were especially characteristic of his fellow-citizens and his epoch. His pictures of shows and circuses, and boating-parties and picnics down the Seine, testify to the delight he took in the enjoyments of the people. There is a zest about them which is more than the detached observer's. Like many others of the painters of his time, he worked also on the Normandy coast, mostly choosing lighthouses and breakwaters for his subject. On these he displayed his manner in its most persuasive and least sensational aspect, attaining harmonies of colour, which, for all the novelty of their method, have a classic calm and finality."

Plate 4

PICASSO: La Vie

Reproduced by courtesy of Messrs. Alex. Reid & Lefevre Ltd.

Pablo Picasso (1881-   )

Pablo Picasso was born at Malaga, the son of a drawing master named Ruiz, and later adopted his mother's name. His youth was passed in Barcelona, but he came to Paris in 1900, shortly afterwards settling in that city.

" The canvases of this period are mainly a series of figure-groups, which in form partake at once of the superficially pathetic implications of popular realistic illustration and the deeper tragic symbolism of Spanish religious sculpture. To the compounding of this recipe, however, Picasso added his own gifts. The emaciated anatomies, eloquent of poverty and starvation, are uniformly portrayed in different keys of blue, which gave to the painting of this time the name of the Blue Period, and of which La Vie *is a fine example. The amount of expression which Picasso evoked from the use of this one colour was the first distinct manifestation of his genius. He handled it with such virtuosity, varying its tone from the light and diaphanous to the deepest possible shade, that there was no monotony in its employment. It speaks and does duty for other colours as well. Later, Picasso was to say, not altogether in jest, that if he found a tube of colour lacking from his paint-box in the course of a picture, he could equally well substitute another for it. The Blue Period is more than a hint at such prestidigitation. In appreciating the revolution in form that he was to effect in more recent stages of development, his wonderful talent as a colourist is not always sufficiently regarded."*

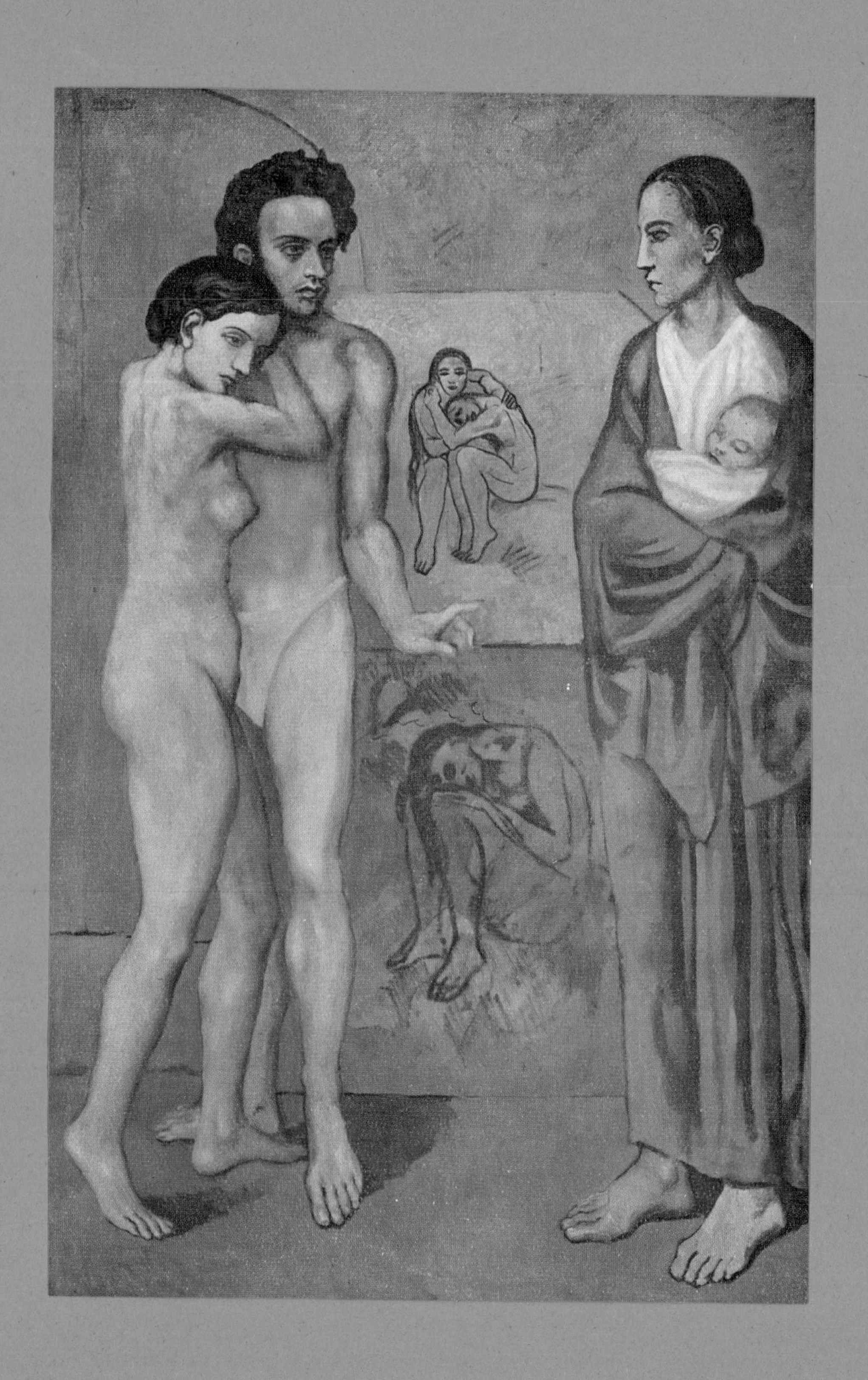

Plate 5

PICASSO: Le Tapis Rouge

Reproduced by courtesy of Mons. Paul Rosenberg

Pablo Picasso (1881-   )

" *In a later phase, the third-dimensional element is abandoned in favour of the purely decorative surface qualities of these geometric figures. Afterwards, still remaining superficial, but founded on more associations with actuality, came a series of tables covered with stuffs falling in a wilderness of cylindrical folds and supporting a mass of heterogeneous "properties"—scrolls, bird-cages, busts, dishes of fruit—all woven into a sternly controlled austerity of design, yet bristling with pictorial incident. Then, as in the splendid* Le Tapis Rouge, *this arrangement took on cubical content and was infused with a glowing wealth of various colour.*"

" *Picasso is not only the inventor of a pictorial treatment of the shapes of natural appearances ; he is an inventor of shape itself. To design, merely as design, he has brought new strength by giving it new foundations ; for art he has conquered a fresh world of wonder and excitement by insisting on the painter's right to create his own form.*"

Plate 6

BRAQUE: Composition avec Fruits

Reproduced by courtesy of Mons. Paul Rosenberg

Georges Braque (1882-   )

Georges Braque was born at Argenteuil, and has exhibited at the Salon des Indépendants *since* 1905.

" Braque, keeping for the most part to a restrained scale of greens and greys, has applied the Cubist analysis into third-dimensional elements to statuesque, sibylline female figures, and multiplied delightful still-life panels of fruit and flowers. There is a sameness verging on monotony in a collection of his work, which is not relieved by his never departing really far from representation ; although such variation as he evolves from a deliberate paucity of theme compels admiration. The pictures are more comprehensive singly than in numbers ; their discipline and grasp of pattern can then be appreciated better. As Picasso is the romantic, so Braque is the classic of the movement."

Plate 7

MATISSE: Femme en Bleu

Collection of the late Mons. Paul Guillaume

Henri Matisse (1869-   )

Henri Matisse was born at Cateau Cambrésis, a small town in Picardy, and gave up a position in a law office to study under Gustave Moreau at the Ecole des Beaux Arts.

" Matisse no longer left the spectator to fill in mentally the blank spaces of his design. He filled them in himself, so that time should not be wasted over them, and with a facility of draughtsmanship that could be as firm and subtle as he wanted, but that he preferred not to elaborate. For as soon as it had become simply divisional in function, that is to say, as soon as it performed the duty of bounding space, he had no more need for it in the picture. All that he sought was an effect of colour and light, both exhibited in their most limpid quality. The spatial relationship, equally with the line, is subordinated to them ; mass, though he could be a master of it when he would, is unimportant ; he adopted representation because, for his aims, he had no need to go beyond it. He painted cliffs fronting the sea, fish, modish women, and odalisques couched in a luxury of tapestries and patterned stuffs. But these forms, indicated with varying degrees of fidelity from realism to vague suggestion, are only an excuse for the pure subjectivity of his colour-harmony. There, the whole gamut of tints is employed with dazzling coruscation. Such painting is remote from time and place ; it is expression in its most clarified essence."

Plate 8

DERAIN: Landscape

Reproduced by courtesy of
Captain Ernest Duveen

André Derain (1880-   )

Derain, born at Chatou, studied in Paris at the Ecole des Beaux Arts*, where he met, and worked with, Matisse.*

" In modern French painting he is the equivalent of Chardin, as Matisse is of Watteau. The one is reason, the other instinct ; and each is a supreme example of two characteristic types of the French spirit. In the end, Derain has yielded to his realism, but he has tempered it with an admirable faculty for selection, and infused it with the spirit of classic tradition. In this he has shown a boldness which has won him from enthusiasts of modernity, whose endeavour has outrun their good intentions, the epithet of " museum-painter." Yet if, in these later days, he has often entered the museums, he has left them again in order to breathe in the sense of actuality, that has been but fortified by the visit. He has not reverted to a tradition that is outworn, but has continued tradition and injected the flame of contemporary life into it. There is a force of reference in his work, but a fine dignity of reserve keeps it in the background, whence it lends authority to Derain's own conservative yet virile style. And this style he has exercised upon still-lifes where, from a limited range of theme and scale of colour, he provides a wealth of pictorial incidents ; on portraits of women in which he has unashamedly invited the beauty of the sitters to collaborate on equal terms with his beauty of treatment, and which are distinguished by notable plastic qualities ; and on Provençal landscapes and woodland scenes where fidelity to the scene wedded to power of selection diffuses over the canvas a charm like that of an early Corot."

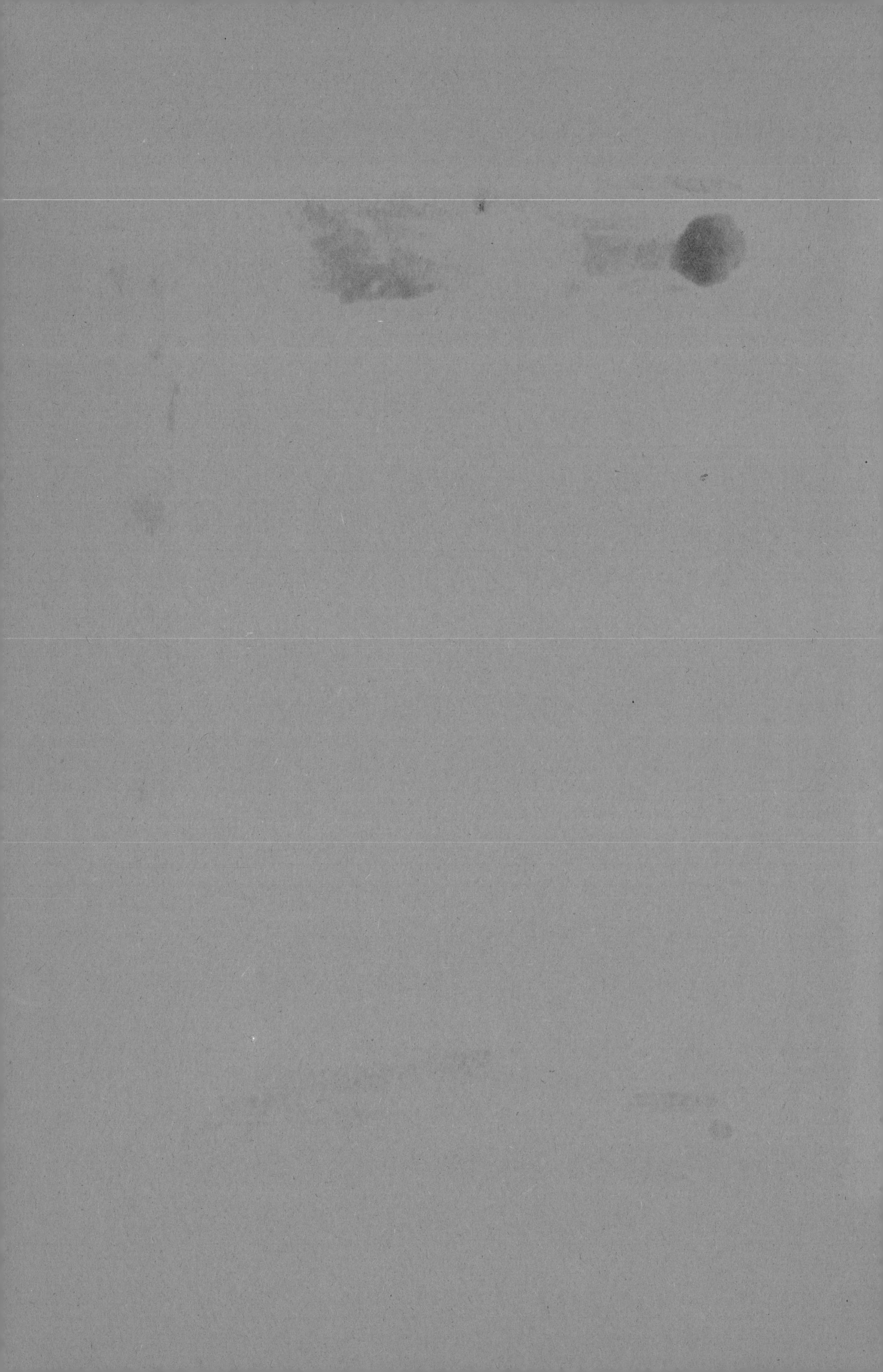

Plate 9

MODIGLIANI: Enfant du Peuple

Collection of the late Mons. Paul Guillaume

Amadeo Modigliani (1884-1920)

Modigliani was an Italian subject, who came to Paris, where he remained until his early death.

" He drew from it [negro sculpture] the essentials of his style in draughtsmanship, and, since he confined himself to portraiture, imprinted its linear characteristics on his sitters. Eyes are reduced to a convention of round or oval, noses elongated and thinned, lips contracted, while as a whole the figure at once joins the category either of etiolation or expansion. There is no middle normal course ; the slightest excess of balance one way or the other is deformed into its particular alternative, just as negro sculpture is either squat and bulky, or extenuated and reed-like. Yet within this intentionally rudimentary convention, Modigliani amazingly conveys likeness, which is saved from caricature by the delicate grace of his lengthened forms, the rich sense of healthy flesh and abundance of his expanded ones. To this sublimation of his design is joined a lustrous clarity of colour. There are no half-tones ; the colour, evenly laid on, is allowed its full force of expression. This enhances the subtle lucidity of his effect, and gives force to the exquisitely attenuated line. The whole figure, according as it falls into one of the two classes, has the equivalent quality in painting of a Gothic or Romanesque arch. And his portraits, confined to a small range of types—Montparnasse friends, servants from the country, and nudes—charmingly self-conscious as they are, with a kind of intellectual naiveté, have the same authority of statement as fine architecture."

modigliani

Plate 10

ROUSSEAU: Landscape

Collection of the late Mons. Paul Guillaume

Henri-Julien Rousseau (1844-1910)

Rousseau was born at Labal, and began to paint in his spare time, while employed by the Octroi de la Ville de Paris.

" Once a member of the French forces sent to Mexico in aid of Maximilian's tragic expedition, Rousseau had come back with a vivid recollection of the luxuriant shapes and colours of the tropical forest. These he carefully portrayed in canvases of a genuine naiveté both of imagination and execution. But he turned his attention also to scenes of contemporary life, in the portraiture of bourgeois groups and landscapes, of the outskirts of Paris. There is a distinct charm in the unforced fidelity of his work, with its absence of all technical trickery."

Plate 11

ROUAULT: Clown

Reproduced by courtesy of The Mayor Gallery, Ltd.

Georges Rouault (1871-   )

Born at Paris, Rouault began his career as a designer of stained glass, and studied under Gustave Moreau at the Ecole des Beaux Arts.

" His painting is a setting of jewels that gleam through darkness, but instead of a grace of form and dreams, he paints the brutal shapes of a barbarous modernity, seeking in contemporary life the savage and truculent expressions of human character. His figures are awkward, with a Romanesque bulk, in their mass ; the line that bounds them is thick and deliberately clumsy. They are, viewed as portraiture, often of a revolting ugliness ; for there is in Rouault a distinct element of harsh satire. But he invests them with a magical depth of colour, a richness of hue that either sparkles dazzlingly, or in whose gloom are lambent tongues of buried fire. Some of the pictures are a devastating exhibition of the nullity and hideousness of the petit bourgeois, others a cry of horror at the degradation of lust ; but there are also robust exultations in the lively, simple joy of fairs and circuses, where colour takes on the stridency of brazen instruments of music, or laughs with the ferocious fun of clowns."

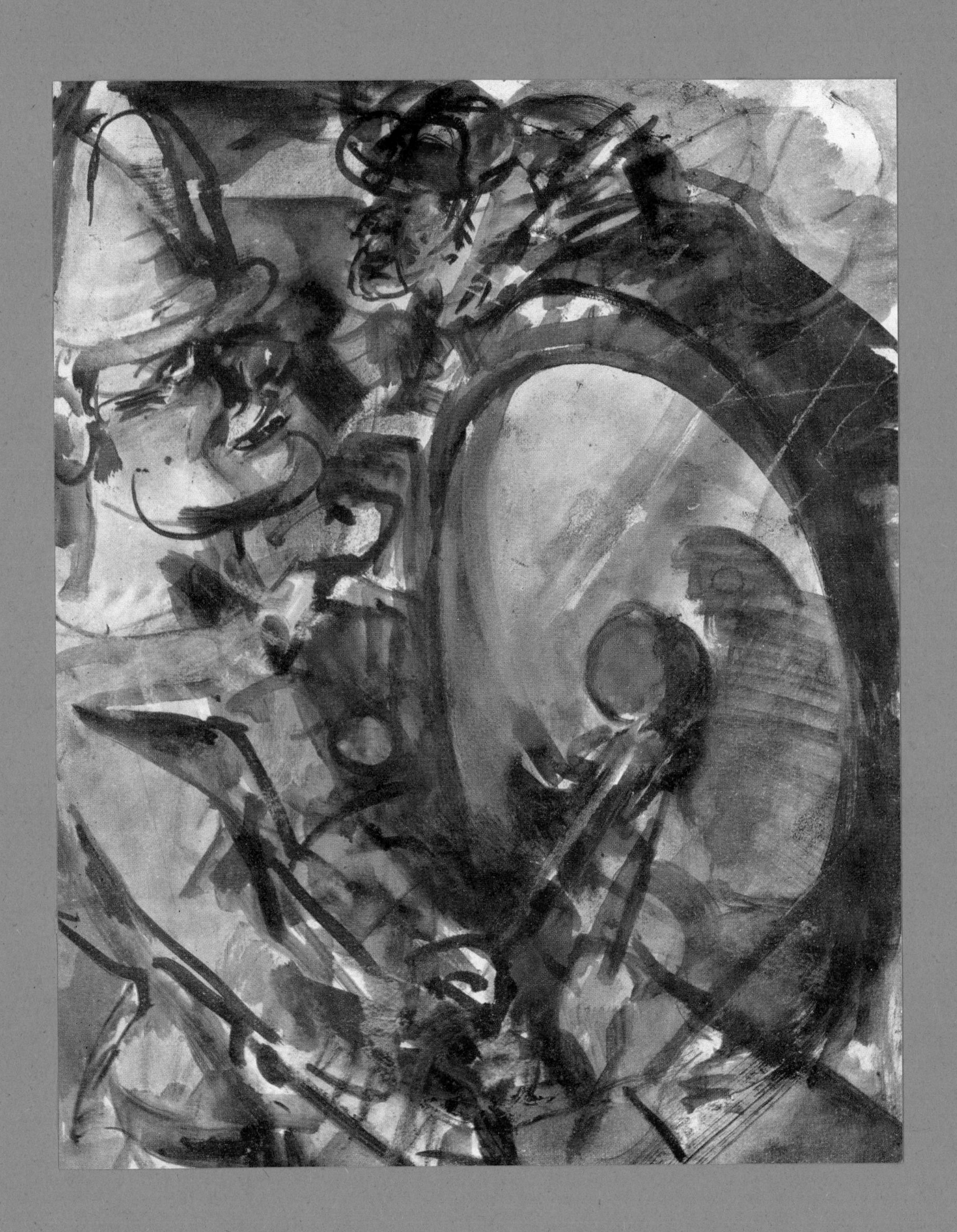

Plate 12

UTRILLO: Le Lapin Agile

Collection of M. Shearman, Esq.

Maurice Utrillo (1883-   )

Born in Paris, Utrillo took the name of a Parisian journalist who adopted him.

" Utrillo was a Fauve in the literary and romantic suggestion that he brought to his work, though technically he was the most classical and traditional painter of the movement. There was nothing very revolutionary about his slightly simplified realism, and the whites, greys and greens of which he was a master from the first are not accentuated above fidelity. Yet their predominance in his work and his constant choice of scenes in which they figure most largely give his pictures an atmosphere all their own. Not only the appearance, but the aura, of certain streets in Montmartre and at the back of Montmartre have been imperishably recorded by Utrillo, and in the sordidness and despair which his presentation of them so poignantly evokes, one may read a personal statement as clear as written autobiography. The enchantment of a lunar region is woven by exquisite harmonies of colour about a region of decaying stones, extenuate greenery and crapulous associations. Never has the Fauvist talent for translating intrinsic ugliness into terms of beauty been so triumphantly exercised.

Plate 13

RENOIR: Baigneuse

Reproduced by courtesy of Die Kunst

Pierre-Auguste Renoir (1841-1920)

Born at Limoges, Renoir *came to Paris while still a child. After being a painter on porcelain and window-blinds, he entered Gleyre's studio, exhibiting for the first time at the Salon of* 1864 *but soon joining his fellow-Impressionists at the* Salon des Refusés. *His later painting was accomplished at Cagnes, behind Nice. It has the properties of substance and roundness which sculpture conveys, but with no frozen immobility. The painting invests his figures with a palpitating energy, flooding them with light and a splendour of colour heightened to its strongest expression. The thickly-clustered foliage, which often gives them a setting, and the running streams in which his bathing groups disport, quiver with the same rhythmic life and communicate* Renoir*'s unabashed sensual delight in visible beauty. His is essentially painting without tears.*

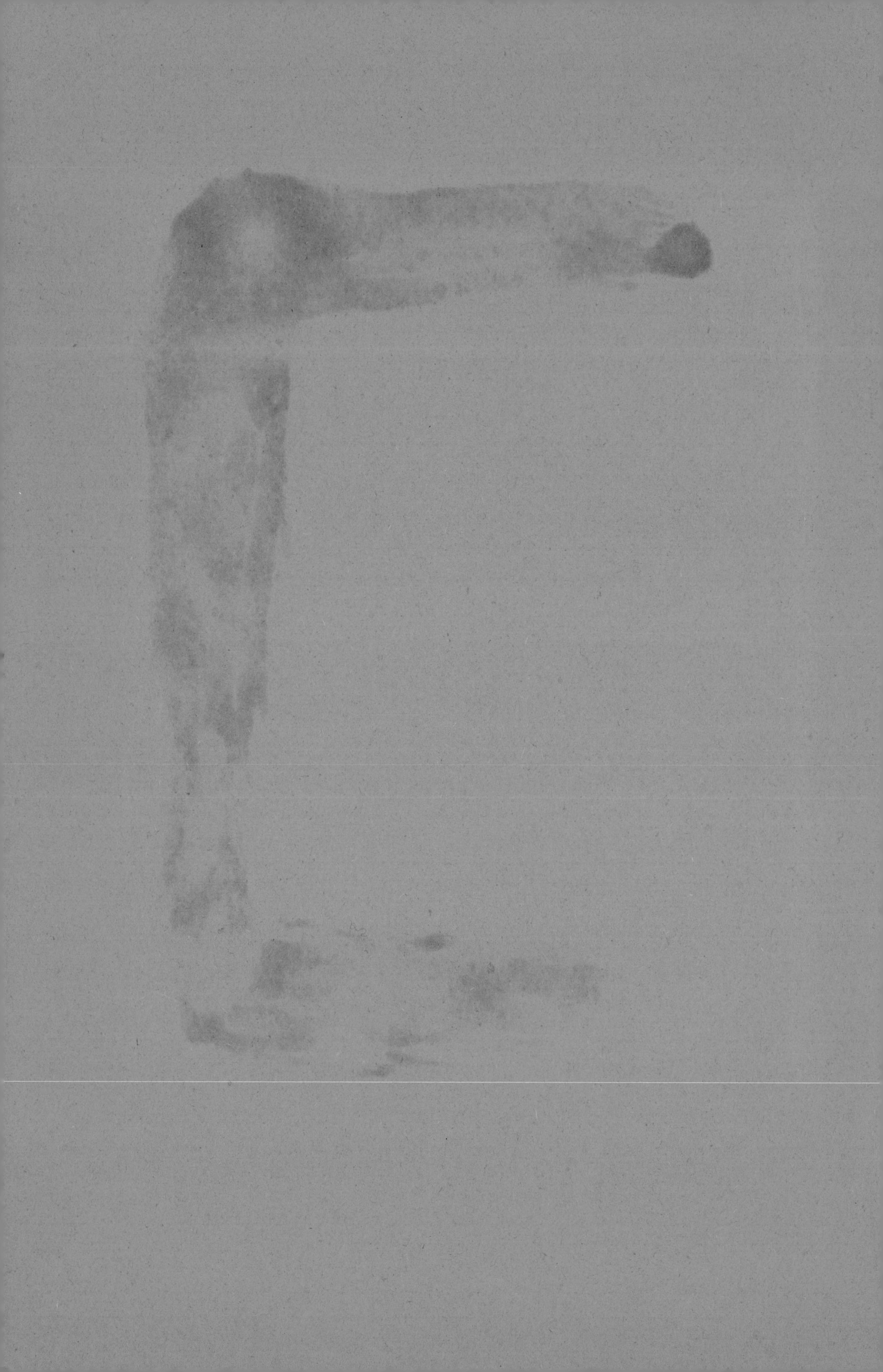

Plate 14

SOUTINE: Choir Boy

Collection of the late Mons. Paul Guillaume

Haim Soutine (1894-   )

Born at Smilovitschi, now part of Lithuania, and settling in Paris shortly after the Russian revolution, Soutine has shown a remarkable adaptability to his environment. Besides his work in still-life, he has seized with amazing keenness the intimate characteristics of the Parisian type of petit bourgeois and employé. The influence of Modigliani is evident in this section of his work, but to that painter's hieratic convention of form he has imparted a fluidity of movement and a very definite turn of humour which sometimes approaches caricature. His colour attains a rare luminosity and the controlled ease of his design has made him a leader among the large band of foreign artists established in the capital and known as the School of Paris in the later manifestations of the modern movement.

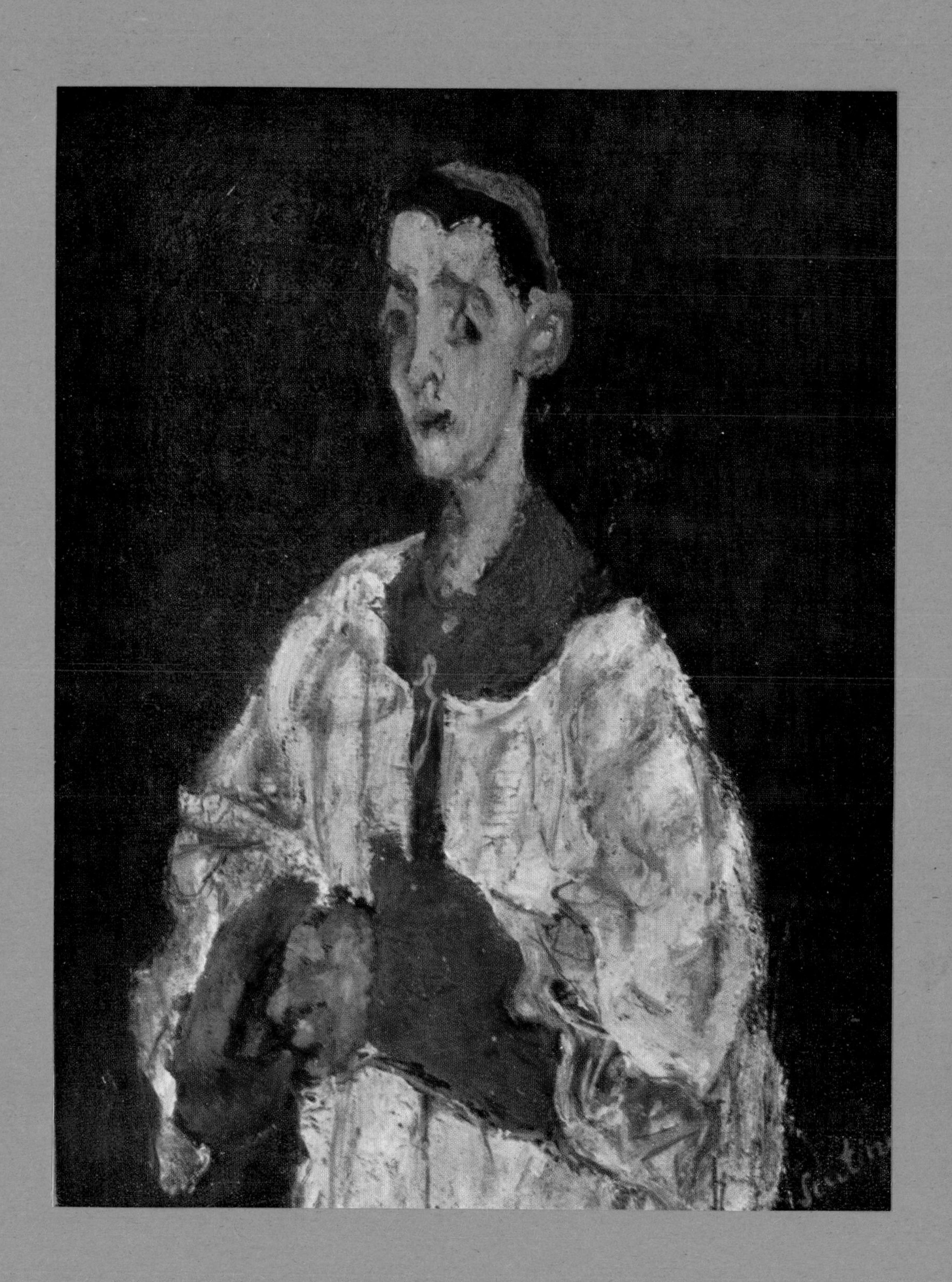

Plate 15

CHAGALL: Flowers and Poet

Reproduced by courtesy of The Mayor Gallery, Ltd.

Marc Chagall (1887-   )

Chagall was born at Witebsk in Russia, and came to Paris in 1910. *He exhibited at the* Salon des Indépendants *from* 1911 *to* 1914. *In the first phase of the Russian revolution he founded a school of painting at Witebsk. In* 1923 *he returned to Paris, but despite his long residence there, his very personal expression in painting retains many native characteristics. He makes an extremely imaginative use of colour, and, with apparent naiveté, reveals the wonders of a fantastic universe of his own creation. Yet the harmony of his compositions is welded in a strong cohesion of rhythm, and a vital sense of poetry keeps them always young and various. He has done much towards giving the later phase of the modern movement its impulse to a picturesque of combined realism and fantasy.*

Marc Chagall

Plate 16

ROY: The Music Room

Reproduced by courtesy of the artist and of Messrs. Wildenstein & Co., Ltd.

Pierre Roy (1880-   )

Roy has for long worked in a direction which has become self-conscious with the advent of the Surrealist School. Without extravagance in presentation he has brought to painting, in the inventive branch of his work, a dream-like quality which is extremely personal. There is a wealth of evocative power in his mysterious figures, playing out the crisis of an unknown drama, and in their strange settings. Technically, he represents natural appearances in a delightful scheme of colour and with a distinction of clear outline ; but these appearances are combined in his vision to construct a world beyond a nature of ordinary visibility. The universe in which his imagination moves is his own personal creation, a kingdom of muted enchantment ; there is a charm of intimate revelation when he lifts the curtain upon it.

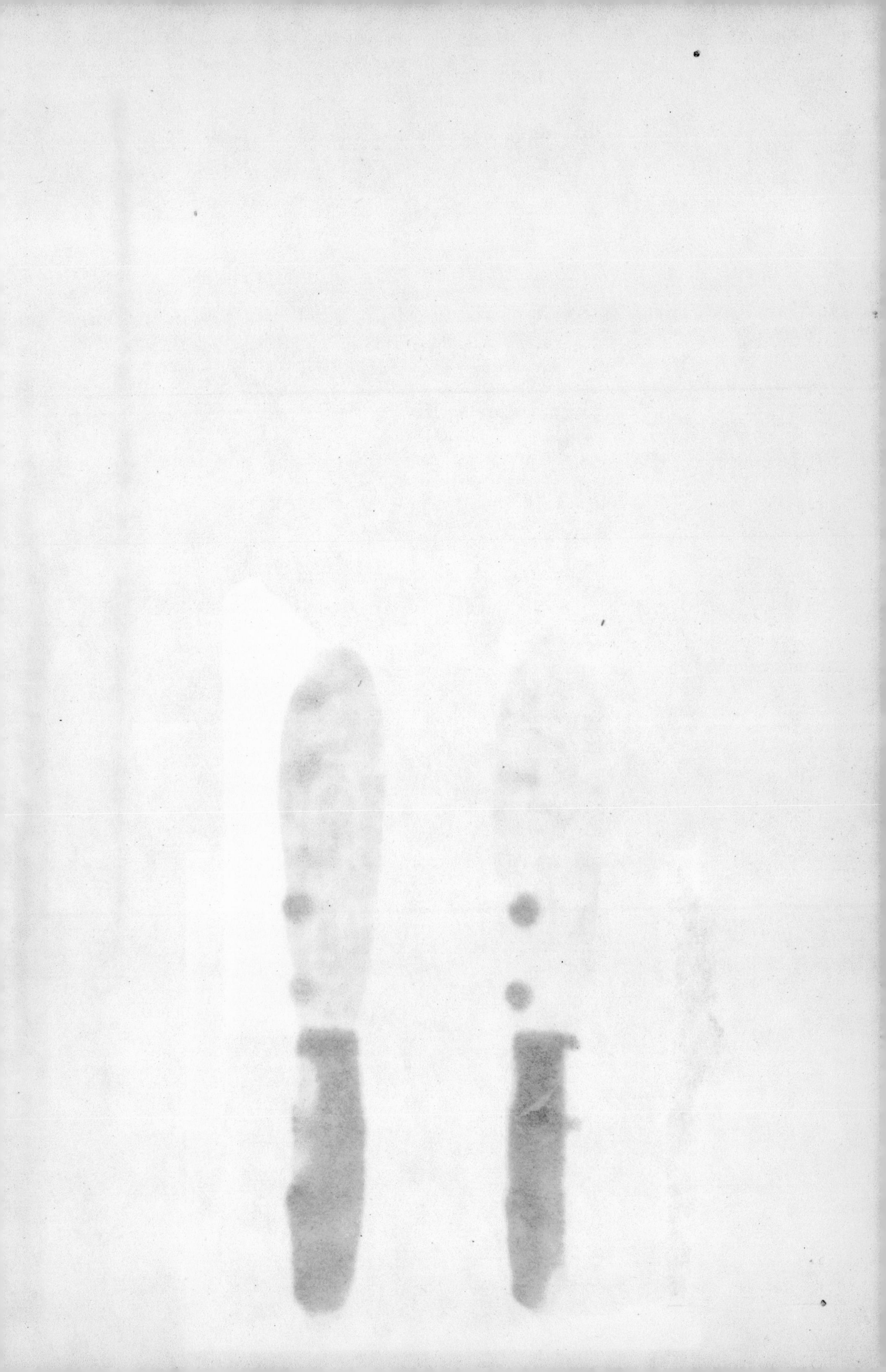

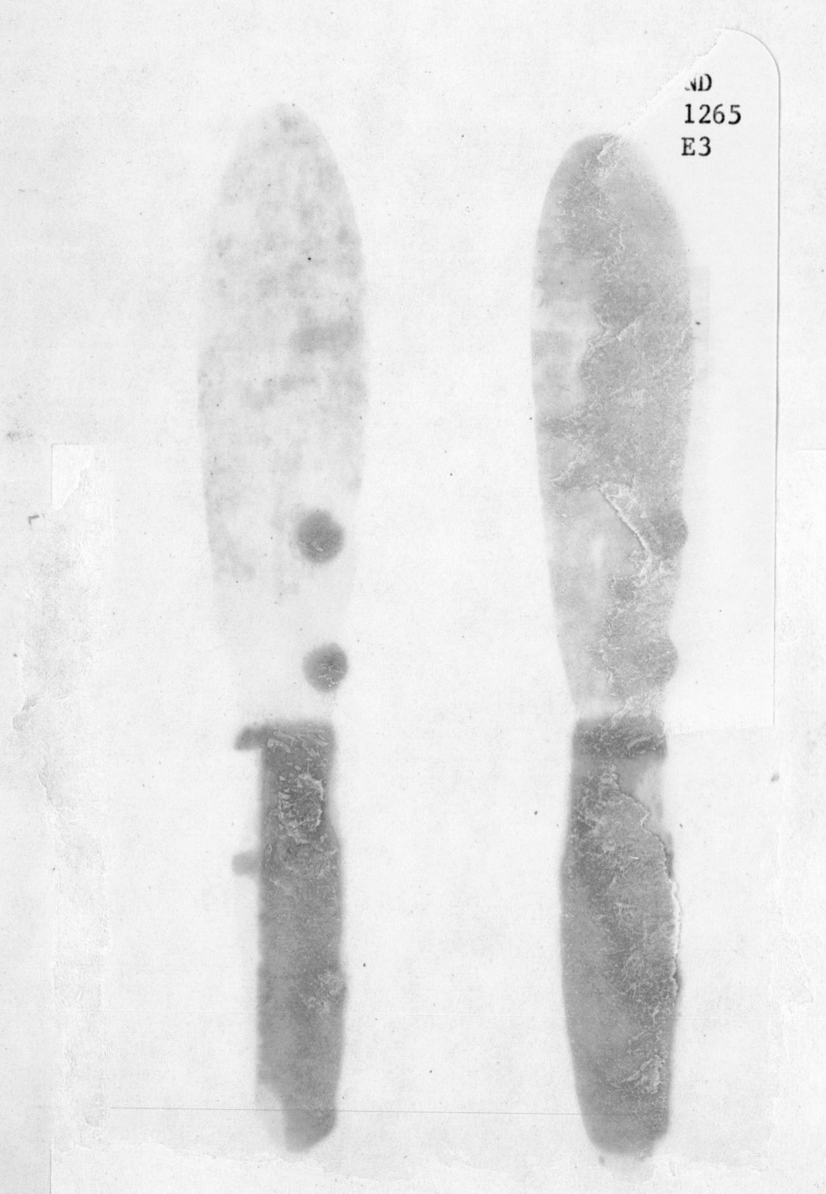

J. S. WESBY & SONS
JAN
1957
Worcester